# Forensic Pattern Recognition

# Forensic Pattern Recognition
## From Fingerprints to Toolmarks

**ROBERT D. KEPPEL**
*Seattle University*

**KATHERINE M. BROWN**
*Sam Houston State University*

**KRISTEN WELCH**
*Sam Houston State University*

PEARSON
Prentice
Hall

Upper Saddle River, New Jersey 07458

**Library of Congress Cataloging-in-Publication Data**

Forensic pattern recognition : from fingerprints to toolmarks / Robert D. Keppel,
Katherine M. Brown & Kristen Welch, editors.
    p.  cm.
Includes bibliographical references.
ISBN 0-13-232948-4
1. Footprints–Identification. 2. Fingerprints–Identification. 3. Tires–Identification.
4. Pattern perception. 5. Criminal investigation. 6. Forensic sciences.
I. Keppel, Robert D. II. Brown, Katherine M. III. Welch, Kristen.
HV8077.5.F6F67 2008
363.25′62—dc22                                           2006026287

**Editor-in-Chief:** Vernon R. Anthony
**Senior Acquisitions Editor:** Tim Peyton
**Associate Editor:** Sarah Holle
**Marketing Manager:** Adam Kloza
**Editorial Assistant:** Jillian Allison
**Production Editor:** Melissa Westley, Carlisle Editorial Services
**Production Liaison:** Barbara Marttine Cappuccio
**Managing Editor:** Mary Carnis
**Manufacturing Manager:** Ilene Sanford
**Manufacturing Buyer:** Cathleen Petersen
**Senior Design Coordinator:** Mary Siener
**Cover Designer:** Diana Hahn
**Cover Images:** Firing impression, Courtesy of Ronald Welsh, Bureau of Forensic Services,
Central Valley Laboratory, Ripon, CA.; Shoe print, Andy Crawford, Dorling Kindersley Media
Library; Tire track, Naoki Okamoto, Getty Images
**Formatting:** Carlisle Publishing Services
**Printing and Binding:** Command Web

Pearson Education Ltd.                          Pearson Education North Asia Ltd.
Pearson Education Singapore, Pte. Ltd.          Pearson Educación de Mexico, S.A. de C.V.
Pearson Education Canada, Ltd.                  Pearson Education Malaysia, Pte. Ltd.
Pearson Education—Japan                         Pearson Education, Upper Saddle River, NJ
Pearson Education Australia PTY, Limited

10 9 8 7 6 5 4 3 2 1
ISBN: 0-13-232948-4

# Contents

# Preface

*The call came in early in the day, before the second cup of coffee could be downed. A truck driver leaving the parking lot of a local topless bar had spotted a body in a field off the nearly deserted feeder road, ten miles from the interstate exit. The call had been convincing, and dispatch sent two cars. The truck driver had been reluctant to enter the field and examine the scene, electing to remain in his truck until the first car arrived. It was obvious that the woman was dead even from the road.*

*As the first responder on the scene, you question the driver and discover that the set of prints leading to and from the body to the road are not his. It had snowed the afternoon and night before and the day was overcast, threatening rain. The shoe pattern in the three-inch mixture of snow and mud is quite distinct. The team leader quickly develops a plan for processing the scene with an eye on the rapidly darkening sky. More officers arrive, tasks are assigned, and a grid search of the surrounding area begins. Two officers are assigned to process the body and a call is made to the medical examiner's office. Your task is to document, process, and collect the shoeprints in the snow. As you are checking your camera and deciding how best to begin, the first drop of rain hits your face. You look overhead and realize that you do not have much time to decide the best technique to lift the print. What is the best technique and medium to use?*

In the perfect crime scene scenario, the officers or crime scene investigators would have plenty of time to call the crime lab and receive advice on the best techniques and materials to use for a given situation. They also have all of the needed materials and extra prints to practice on. Unfortunately, the crime scene scenario, as well as the investigation, is not perfect. Not all police departments have a team of crime scene investigators to call in, fully equipped crime scene kits with the latest equipment or materials, or access to a professional crime lab at a moment's notice. Things never seem to fall seamlessly or quickly in place as movies and television shows, such as *CSI*, suggest.

Investigators have to think quickly on their feet, and diligently stay abreast of emerging techniques and developments in their field. Preparation and practice goes a long way. Many investigators take classes and train for crime scene investigation, processing, and analysis. The best investigators read extensively about advancements and the best practices in their field. They also dedicate the time to practice the different techniques and procedures to determine the best methods to process and collect various types of evidence. However, there will always be a situation or a piece of evidence that leaves even the most experienced investigators in doubt as to how best to process and collect it.

This book has been designed and developed as a resource for students, officers, and investigators. It is both a laboratory exercise guide and a quick reference tool in the field for recognizing, identifying, processing, and analyzing pattern evidence. The techniques provided in the book were researched and performed by students from Sam Houston State University's Master of Science in Forensic Science Program. Each of the five chapters provides an in-depth look at pattern evidence and analysis, including background information and standard procedures for lifting and casting various prints.

Chapter 1 provides an overview of fingerprint evidence. Authors Kathleen Born and Monica Brady provide a brief history of fingerprinting and its origin. This chapter highlights the procedures for the classification, examination, and lifting of fingerprints. Several techniques are introduced on the collection and preservation of latent and patent fingerprints, including physical lifting and visualization techniques, chemical lifting and visualization techniques, fuming procedures, and assorted techniques for collecting and preserving fingerprint evidence in unusual situations.

Chapter 2 provides an introduction and overview of shoe impressions. Authors Amy Carlson and Jamie Lee focus on the identification of various footwear and methods to successfully lift different types of footwear impressions. Procedures for collecting and preserving three-dimensional impression evidence and collecting known standards are discussed. An often overlooked or forgotten piece of evidence, shoe impression evidence can be very useful in tying offenders to a crime scene and revealing the course of events.

Chapter 3 details the methods for collecting and preserving tire impressions. Authors Ryan Mudd and James Warkentine provide an overview on the identification of tread patterns and lifting procedures for collecting tire impressions. Information is included on collecting known standards for comparison. Tire impressions can be a valuable piece of evidence for investigators, if they are properly identified, collected, and preserved at the crime scene.

Chapter 4 highlights the importance of recognizing and identifying bite marks. Authors Stephanie Rollins and Wendi Sanders provide an introduction to forensic odontology and reveal the important role of dentists in identifying, documenting, and collecting bite mark evidence. Bite marks can be a very revealing and unique piece of evidence linking offenders to victims and crime scenes.

Chapter 5 provides an overview of toolmark evidence. Toolmarks are an interesting source of evidence at crime scenes. Authors Sharla McCloskey and Anna Leggett describe procedures for identifying and processing toolmark evidence. Toolmarks and impressions can be left on various types of surfaces by various objects and can be very useful sources of evidence. Information is also provided on the most likely places and surfaces to look for toolmarks and the procedure for casting toolmarks.

# Editors

**Robert D. Keppel, Ph.D.,** is a visiting professor of Criminal Justice at Seattle University. He spent two years as an associate professor at Sam Houston State University. He retired after 17 years as the Chief Criminal Investigator with the Washington State Attorney General's Office. He has more than 29 years of homicide investigation experience. Among his many homicide investigation experiences, he has been a consultant to the Atlanta Police on the Missing and Murdered Children's Cases, a member of the national planning committee for the Violent Criminal Apprehension Program (VICAP) and a consultant to the Green River Murders Task Force, Seattle, Washington. He also served as a consultant to the El Paso Police Department in the Desert Area serial murders in Texas, the Austin Police Department in the Yogurt Shop murders, the Jefferson Parish Sheriff's Department in the New Orleans area prostitute murders, the Santa Barbara Sheriff's Office in the Nightstalker murder cases in California, and to the Oregon State Police in the Randy Kraft murders in Oregon.

Dr. Keppel is the founder of the Washington State Homicide Investigation and Tracking System (HITS) that set the benchmark for how police handle information in support of homicide investigations. He was the project director for a federal grant from Bureau of Justice assistance (BJA) entitled, "Managing Investigative Technologies," which was completed in 2002. He was the project director for an Office of Juvenile Justice and Delinquency Prevention (OJJDP) grant entitled, "Investigative Case Management for Missing Children Homicides," which was completed in 1997. He was the project director for a National Institute of Justice grant entitled, "Improving the Investigation of Homicide and the Apprehension Rate of Murderers," which was completed in 1989. He was the primary investigator for the King County Sheriff's Department in the Ted Bundy murder cases in the Pacific Northwest and was present for Bundy's final confessions before his Florida execution. He has personally investigated, reviewed, or consulted in more than 2000 murder cases. He has lectured extensively to police officers at national seminars on homicide investigation. He has testified in trial as an expert on the method of operation of serial killers, the "signature aspects" of murder investigations and police investigations.

Dr. Keppel is the author of several articles and five books entitled: *The Psychology of Serial Killer Investigations*, published in 2003 by Academic Press; *The Riverman: Ted Bundy and I Hunt the Green River Killer*, published in 1995 by Pocket Books, New York, NY; *Signature Killers*, published in 1997 by Pocket Books, New York, NY; *Murder: A Multidisciplinary Anthology of Readings*, published in 1999 by Harcourt Brace, Orlando, FL; *Serial Murder: Future Implications for Police Investigations*, published in 2000 by Authorlink.com.

Dr. Keppel received his Doctor of Philosophy degree in criminal justice from the University of Washington in 1992. He graduated from Washington State University with a Bachelor of Science degree in police science and administration in 1966 and a Master of Arts degree in police science and administration in 1967. Also, he received a Master of Education degree from Seattle University in 1979.

**Katherine M. Brown, M.A.,** received her Bachelor of Arts degree in government with a minor in sociology from the University of Texas at Austin and her Master of Arts degree in criminal justice and criminology from Sam Houston State University and is currently finishing her doctorate in criminal justice at the same institution. Ms. Brown's research interests include child abduction murder investigation, crime scene investigation, serial murder, offender profiling, forensic evidence, and other solvability factors affecting murder investigations. Her prior experience includes employment in Texas state government and the legal field. Prior to graduate school, Ms. Brown was the owner and founder of a successful marketing consulting business. Ms. Brown served as the assistant to the director of the Forensic Science Program at Sam Houston State University.

**Kristen Welch, M.A.,** received her Bachelor of Arts degree from Texas A&M University in political science with a minor in sociology. She received her Master of Arts degree in criminal justice and criminology from Sam Houston State University and is currently finishing her doctorate in criminal justice at the same institution. Ms. Welch's research interests include criminological theory, racial profiling, crime scene investigation, serial murder, offender profiling, victimology, sentencing disparities, indigent defense, forensic evidence and other solvability factors affecting murder investigations. Currently Ms. Welch teaches Criminology, Research Methods, and Criminal Justice courses at Sam Houston State University College of Criminal Justice.

# Contributors

**Kathleen M. Born** received her Bachelor of Science degree in biomedical science from Texas A&M University. Ms. Born worked for six years for two contractors with the National Aeronautics and Space Administration (NASA) in coordinating positions. She is currently working on her Master of Science in forensic science at Sam Houston State University.

**Monica L. Brady** received her Bachelor of Science in biology and chemistry at West Texas A&M University. While pursuing her undergraduate degree, she gained experience with the Women's Health Research Institute of Amarillo, a research lab at Texas Tech University School of Pharmacy in Amarillo, Texas. While there, she performed research for "*Inhibiting Long-Chain Fatty Acyl CoA Synthetase Does Not Increase Agonist-Induced Release of Arachidonate Metabolites from Human Endothelial Cells*," which was subsequently published in the *Journal of Vascular Research*. Ms. Brady is currently working on her Master of Science degree in forensic science at Sam Houston State University.

**Amy Carlson** graduated from Brigham Young University with a Bachelor of Science degree in biochemistry in 2003. Her experience includes employment in an analytical laboratory for two years testing herbal supplements using specialized equipment; gas chromatography, spectroscopy, and high performance liquid chromatography. Ms. Carlson is currently working on her Master of Science degree in forensic science at Sam Houston State University.

**Jamie Lee** is currently enrolled in the Master of Science in forensic science program at Sam Houston State University. She holds a Bachelor of Science degree in biology with a minor in chemistry from Sam Houston State University. In addition to her coursework, Ms. Lee is employed part-time as a bookkeeper/assistant service manager.

**Anna K. Leggett** is currently a student at Sam Houston State University enrolled in Master of Science in forensic science program. She is a graduate of Texas A&M University in College Station, where she received her Bachelor of Science degree in chemistry. Ms. Leggett's interest in forensic science was sparked by her high school chemistry teacher who inspired her to work toward her goal.

**Sharla McCloskey** received her Bachelor of Science degree in chemistry and mathematics from Wayland Baptist University. While in attendance there she was employed as a teaching assistant for the undergraduate chemistry and physics laboratories. Ms. McCloskey also participated in the planning and execution of the Teacher Quality Grant Programs funded by the Texas Higher Education Coordinating Board of Texas and carried out at WBU. She is currently enrolled in the Master of Science in forensic science program at Sam Houston State University with an interest in toxicology.

**Ryan D. Mudd** received his Bachelor of Science degree in biomedical science from Texas A&M University. While pursuing his degree, he was employed under Dr. Robert Hildreth in the undergraduate organic chemistry labs. Mr. Mudd also worked as a teaching assistant in an undergraduate microbiology lab under the supervision of Dr. Charles Scanlan. Currently, he is pursuing a Master of Science in forensic science degree at Sam Houston State University.

**Stephanie Rollins** graduated from Hardin Simmons University in Abilene, Texas with a Bachelor of Science degree in biology and chemistry. While there, she served as a research assistant in the chemistry department and also participated in an internship for the Abilene Police Department's criminal investigation division, primarily focusing on fingerprint evidence. Ms. Rollins is currently pursuing a Master of Science in forensic science degree from Sam Houston State University.

**Wendi Sanders** graduated from Texas A&M University with a Bachelor of Science degree with a major in biomedical science and a minor in history. Ms. Sanders' experience included employment at the Human Genome Sequencing Center at the Baylor College of Medicine in Houston. Her work consisted of mapping and sequencing all types of DNA including: the human genome project, monkey DNA, and starfish DNA. Ms. Sanders is currently pursuing her Master of Science degree in forensic science at Sam Houston State University.

**James Warkentine** received his Bachelor of Science in forensic anthropology from Baylor University. His experience includes an internship in forensic entomology. Mr. Warkentine was a member of the golden key club and an active member of Baylor's forensic team. Mr. Warkentine continued his education in chemistry at the University of Texas San Antonio where he worked for one year in an analytical lab. He is currently working on his Master of Science in forensic science degree at Sam Houston State University.

# Forensic Pattern Recognition

# 1

# Fingerprints

Kathleen M. Born and Monica Brady

## Introduction

Fingerprint evidence is one of the most important pieces of the crime scene investigation. Fingerprints are defined as imprints deposited on a surface by the friction ridges on a fingertip. Fingerprints can be used to identify people because they are completely unique to every individual. Fingerprints are formed in the womb and never change throughout life with the exception of scarring; however, they will grow larger as the individual matures (Ashbaugh 1999).

### History of Fingerprints

Fingerprints have a long history dating back to the seventeenth century. Knowledge of this history is a key element to proving the integrity of fingerprint evidence in court. A summary timeline of the history of fingerprints is shown as follows.

| | |
|---|---|
| **1641–1712 ▲** | **Nehemiah Grew**—first scientist to publish detailed drawings of ridge patterns |
| **1781–1869 ▲** | **Johannes Evangelista Purkinje**—wrote a thesis describing fingerprint patterns and friction ridge details |
| **1833–1917 ▲** | **Sir William Herschel**—first European to correlate fingerprints to identifying individuals and routinely used fingerprints to help control fraud in false impersonations and contracts |
| **1843–1930 ▲** | **Dr. Henry Faulds**—began a collection of fingerprints and was the first person to solve a crime by the use of fingerprint evidence |

**1822–1917 ▲**    ***Sir Francis Galton***—first scientist to classify the minutiae on the fingerprints in his book, *Finger Prints*, which established the uniqueness and permanence of fingerprints

**1855–1925 ▲**    ***Juan Vucetich***—helped solve a murder in Argentina with the use of fingerprints

**1850–1931 ▲**    ***Sir Edward Henry***—developed a fingerprint classification system called the Henry System which is detailed in his book, *Classification and Uses of Fingerprints.* (Henry 1913)

**1903 ▲**    United States prisons and some police departments introduced fingerprinting into their processing of prisoners and criminal records

**1910 ▲**    ***Jennings Case***—fingerprint identification was the primary evidence used to convict Thomas Jennings in a landmark case in Chicago. (James and Norby 2005; Lee and Gaensslen 2001)

The United States now uses a modified Henry system as a method for classification of 10-print cards for one individual. The 10-print card process consists of inking and rolling each fingertip and fingers in individual spaces on the card (as shown in Figure 1.1). The upper prints are impressions of each finger taken individually. The fingers are rolled from side to side to obtain the entire ridge detail. The lower prints are smaller impressions which are taken by simultaneously printing all the fingers of each hand, excluding the thumb. The thumb is printed separately from the other fingers. All of the lower prints are pressed impressions that are not rolled, but pressed straight down. Figure 1.2 shows an example of a 10-print card that was poorly prepared. Notice how the rolled fingerprints are not a complete representation of the full ridge detail, and the bottom right and left boxes cut off the fingerprints of the little fingers on both hands.

### Types of Fingerprints

There are three different types of fingerprints found at crime scenes: latent prints, patent (or visible) prints, and plastic (or impression) prints. A *latent print* is defined as an impression that is not readily visible to the naked eye and requires further developing to enhance the details. Latent prints are the most common type of fingerprints found at crime scenes. *Patent prints* are fingerprint impressions that are visible due to the medium in which the impression is made. Some common mediums are dirt, grease, blood, or dust. Patent prints do not usually require further developing, but may require

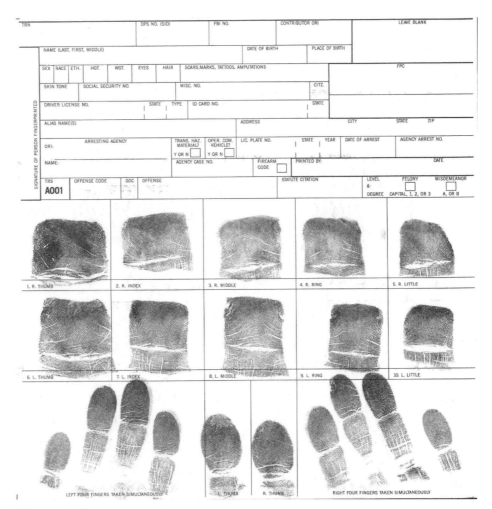

**Figure 1.1** Typical 10-Print Card

additional visualization techniques. *Plastic prints* are recognizable fingerprints made by pressing on a soft receiving surface that will retain a three-dimensional representation of the friction ridge detail. Examples of receiving surfaces include candles, butter, putty, or tar. The methods of enhancing, preserving, and collecting all types of prints are discussed later in this chapter (Federal Bureau of Investigation 1998; James and Norby 2005).

### Composition of Latent Print Residue

Latent fingerprints are made by natural secretions of the skin that are transferred to a surface, leaving an outline of the friction ridges. The surfaces of fingers, hands, and the bottom of feet all have friction ridge skin. This type of skin has pores which contain small secretory glands called *eccrines* that secrete a watery type of sweat onto the skin surface. This sweat from the eccrine glands is the basis for latent fingerprint residue. There are two other types of

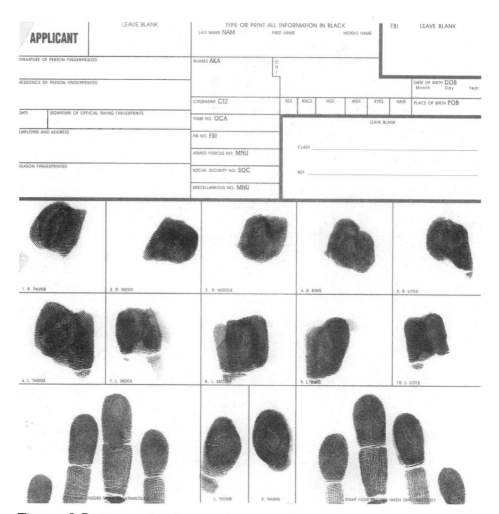

**Figure 1.2**  Example of a Poorly Printed 10-Print Card

secretory glands: apocrine and sebaceous. The apocrine glands are primarily found in armpits and genital areas. The sebaceous glands are found in areas containing hair follicles, such as the face and scalp, and they secrete a sebum-rich deposit that is a heavier, oilier deposit than from the eccrine glands. Latent fingerprint residue most commonly consists of deposits from eccrine and sebaceous glands (Ashbaugh 1999; Lee and Gaensslen 2001).

### Locating and Documenting the Evidence

One of the most important steps in the examination of fingerprint evidence is locating the prints within the crime scene. Examiners should start at the center of the crime scene or at the body and work their way out in a grid-like fashion. Entrance and exit points should always be carefully examined for prints, as well as objects that were disturbed or surfaces that were likely touched during the crime. Specialists should use gloves and handle objects and surfaces carefully so that prints are not obliterated. Plastic and patent prints are sometimes easier to locate since they tend to be more visual than latent. Patent prints can usually be located on dirty or dusty surfaces. Plastic prints can be found on candles, drying paint, and soap. Latent prints are most easily found on smooth, polished surfaces, and are usually located by using oblique lighting. The weapon or weapons used in the crime and their parts should always be carefully examined for prints, including both unfired and spent bullet cartridges. The floors should always be carefully examined for fingerprints or bare footprints. In specific circumstances and under favorable conditions, fingerprints can be found on rougher surfaces such as wood, tightly woven materials, starched fabrics, and human skin. Finally, any loose paper or documents should be thoroughly checked for latent prints. If possible, objects that are suspected of having prints on their surfaces should be collected (Federal Bureau of Investigation 1998; Ruslander 2001).

Documentation is an invaluable tool in crime scene investigations, and it includes recording information, drawing sketches, and photography. All prints should have a record of the exact location and a description of the object the print was located on. In every case, before developing any prints, photographs should be taken using different angles and lighting techniques. This is extremely important because there is always the possibility of obliterating or altering part of the fingerprint detail during the processing. A photograph with a one-to-one scale should be taken of the prints before and after the enhancement techniques prior to lifting (Federal Bureau of Investigation 1998).

### *Fingerprint Patterns and Ridge Characteristics*

There are three well-established premises of friction ridge identification from the book *Scientific Evidence in Criminal Cases* that are used in law enforcement. These premises are stated as follows:

1. The friction ridge patterns that begin to develop during fetal life remain unchanged during life, and even after death, until decomposition destroys the ridged skin.
2. The patterns differ from individual to individual, and even from digit to digit, and are never duplicated in their minute details.
3. Although all patterns are distinct in their ridge characteristics, their overall pattern appearances have similarities which permit a systematic classification of the impressions. (Moenssens, Inbau, and Starrs 1986, p. 421)

Three basic patterns are used to classify fingerprints: the arch, the loop, and the whorl. Each of these classes includes subcategories. The arch can be plain or tented, the loop can be a radial or right slope loop or an ulnar or left slope loop, and the whorl can be a plain whorl, central pocket loop whorl, double loop whorl, or an accidental whorl. Within these fingerprint patterns, there are a number of ridge characteristics or minutiae. These include ridge endings, enclosures, bifurcations, islands, spurs, and crossovers. Figures 1.3 and 1.4 show each of the patterns and their subcategories, as well as the minutiae (Federal Bureau of Investigation 1998; James and Norby 2005).

**Figure 1.3** Examples of Fingerprint Patterns (a). Double Whorl (b). Plain Arch (c). Plain Whorl (d). Radial Slope Loop (e). Tented Arch (f). Ulnar Slope Loop

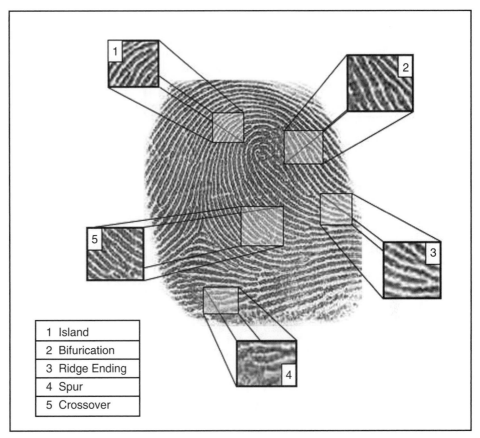

**Figure 1.4**   Examples of Fingerprint Minutiae

# Processing Technique Selection Guide

### *Latent Prints*

**Most nonporous surfaces**

#### *Physical*
Lifting Powder
Luminescent Powder
Magnetic Powder

#### *Chemical*
Iodine Fuming
Iodine Spray Reagent
Cyanoacrylate Fuming
Cyanoacrylate Microburst Method
Acceleration
Enhancement
DFO
PD

### Porous Surfaces
Ninhydrin
Acetone Base
Petroleum Ether Base
PD

### Wet Surfaces
SPR

## Patent Prints

### Blood Prints
Amido Black
Methanol Base
Water base (Fischer)
Coomassie Blue
DAB
LCV
Crowles Double Stain

### Prints Left on Tape
Alternate Black Powder
Ash Gray Powder
Gentian Violet
Sticky-Side Powder
Liqui-Drox

### Prints Left on Currency
PD

### Prints Left on Magazines/Photos
VMD

### Prints Found on Oily/Greasy Surfaces
Sudan Black

### Prints Left on Painted Surfaces
Amido Black (Water Base)

### Prints Left on Human Skin

# Collection and Preservation of Latent Fingerprints

The best place to develop latent prints is in the laboratory; however, sometimes it may be necessary to develop latent prints at crime scenes. If this is done, caution should be taken to ensure that no prints are altered or destroyed. In order to protect the print evidence as much as possible at a crime scene, photographs should be taken both before and after processing. Examination of all print evidence with a laser or special light source should also be done before any processing/development of the prints is performed. Also, it is best to always make a test print to determine the best procedure/ technique to use before lifting the actual print. Processing techniques vary depending on the type of surface the print was left on as well as the residue of the latent print, including perspiration, blood, oil or grease, and dust. The condition of the surface, characteristics including dryness, wetness, dirtiness, and tackiness or stickiness, also contributes to determining the correct processes. Following are the most commonly used fingerprint-lifting techniques.

**At all times remember:**

- Wearing gloves is extremely important.
- All lifts should be documented for later identification.
- Not all fingerprints are readily visible so all objects suspected of bearing fingerprints should be treated as though they have fingerprints on them.
- **Crime scene fingerprints are perishable!**

## Physical Lifting/Visualization Techniques

Latent fingerprints are usually visualized and lifted using fine particles, such as powders, to create a contrast between the print and the background it was left on. These are commonly referred to as *physical methods*, usually defined as lifting methods that do not involve any chemicals or reactions.

### Powder Dusting

Powdering is the application of finely ground, colored powder to a nonporous object to make latent prints visible. Powder clings to moisture, oil, and other residues. Regular powders consist of both a resinous polymer for adhesion and a colorant for contrast. There are many types of commercially available colored and metallic powder. Those most commonly used include black fingerprint powder, manganese dioxide powder, lampblack powder, white fingerprint powder, chalk titanium oxide powder, gray fingerprint powder, and magnetic powder. All nonmagnetic powders have the same basic procedures (Trozzi, Schwartz, and Hollars 2000).

### Luminescent Powders

Luminescent powders are useful for processing prints found on surfaces that present a contrast problem if developed with regular powder. They allow better results upon examination with ultraviolet light or laser examination (Lee and Gaensslen 2001, p. 112).

Things to consider when choosing a powder:

- The surface the print is on should be suitable for powder dusting and not attractive to the powder itself.

- The color selected should provide maximum contrast with the surface the print is on.
- The powder must adhere well to the deposits left by the friction ridges.
- The particle size should be fine enough to yield clear, well defined patterns. (Lee and Gaensslen 2001, p. 110)

**Steps for developing prints using powder dusting[1]:**

1. Select an appropriate powder and brush to use for lifting.
2. Pour needed amount of powder into a small pile.
3. Apply powder to the brush by lightly touching the powder surface and tapping brush on finger to remove excess.
4. Place brush over print and either spin brush between fingers or lightly tap brush to deposit powder onto latent print. If necessary, lightly brush the powder onto the print, brushing in the direction of any ridges that begin to appear.
5. Build powder onto ridges and stop when latent print reaches point of sufficient clarity.
6. Clean excess powder from between ridges using brush or cotton.
7. Use cotton to process large areas by dipping cotton into powder and lightly wiping over the surface. When outline of the latent print becomes visible, stop using the cotton and switch to the brush to complete the development.
8. Photograph the developed print.
9. Apply a suitable fingerprint-lifting tape carefully. The tape should cover approximately one inch on either side of the latent. Start by pressing the tape down before the margin of the print. Slowly press it down, working back and forth across the face to ensure no air bubbles get trapped. After tape is applied to area, carefully peel the tape off the surface, lifting the print with it.
10. Transfer the tape to a transparent or contrasting colored card, once again making sure that there are no air bubbles trapped under the tape. (Trozzi, Schwartz, and Hollars 2000, p. 26)

## Magnetic Powders

Magnetic powders are useful on surfaces such as plastics and leather and are especially beneficial when examination of vertical surfaces, such as walls, is required (Lee and Gaensslen 2001, p. 112).

**Steps for developing prints using magnetic powder:**

1. Place magna brush wand with magnet engaged into container of magnetic powder. This will produce a bristle-like effect at the end of the wand when withdrawn.

---

[1] As with any other laboratory procedure, care should be taken to prevent injury and health hazards. Follow common laboratory safety procedures and refer to MSDS when needed.

2. Apply in a circular motion to the surface being examined. Make sure that only the magnetic powder touches the surface, not the wand.
3. After the print has been developed, hold the wand over the container and withdraw the control rod. This will disengage the magnet and release the powder.
4. Reengage the magnet and pass the clean wand over the developed latent print and the surrounding area to remove excess powder. Do not touch the surface. (Trozzi, Schwartz, and Hollars 2000, p. 26)

## Chemical Lifting/Visualization Techniques

Latent fingerprints may also be lifted using chemical methods. *Chemical lifting* refers to the use of liquid solutions in visualizing prints that are very difficult to develop using physical methods (powders). Chemical lifting usually employs the use of specific reagents and rinses to develop and analyze a latent print.

### Iodine Fuming

Iodine fuming interacts with the ridge components, leaving a dirty-brown colored appearance or with grease or oils on porous surfaces leaving a yellow stain.

**Note: Latent prints developed with iodine fumes must be photographed immediately.**

### Iodine Fuming Cabinet Method

#### Equipment

Fuming chamber, ceramic or glass dish, heat source

#### Procedure

1. Place iodine crystals in the ceramic or glass dish.
2. Place the specimen to be processed in the fuming chamber.
3. Apply heat to the crystals and observe development.
4. Remove the specimen(s) from the chamber when sufficient development has occurred. (Trozzi, Schwartz, and Hollars 2000, p. 31)

### Iodine Spray Reagent

Iodine spray reagent or liquid iodine is used to develop latent prints on porous or nonporous specimens.

#### Mixing Procedure

The iodine spray reagent process consists of two solutions—the iodine and the fixer—from which a working solution is prepared.

### Solution A (Iodine)

| | |
|---|---|
| Iodine crystals | 1 g |
| Cyclohexane | 1000 mL |

Mix on a stirring device for approximately 30 minutes.

### Solution B (Fixer)

| | |
|---|---|
| α-Naphthoflavone | 5 g |
| Methylene chloride | 40 mL |

Mix manually until all the α-naphthoflavone is dissolved. Solutions A and B are stock solutions that are combined to make a working solution.

### Working Solution

Add 2 mL of Solution B for every 100 mL of Solution A. These ingredients must be placed on a stirring device and mixed thoroughly for 5 minutes. After mixing the solution, it must be filtered into a beaker or directly into the sprayer. The filters can consist of a facial tissue, paper towel, filter paper, or any other material that will allow liquid to pass freely.

### Procedure

When spraying iodine spray reagent, the finest mist possible is the most effective method of application. If the spray is heavy, it will overdevelop the area being processed. An artist-type air brush is very effective in this process (Trozzi, Schwartz, and Hollars 2000, p. 32).

## *Cyanoacrylate Fuming*

Used for development on surfaces such as plastics, electrical tape, garbage bags, Styrofoam, carbon paper, aluminum foil, finished and unfinished wood, rubber, copper and other metals, cellophane, rubber bands, and smooth rocks. It is the same thing as Super Glue. **This method proves easier if a test print is placed in the tank or cabinet and watched and used as a "timer" for development**.

### Cyanoacrylate Fuming Procedure

1. Place the object(s) prints into fuming tank or cabinet (any suitable container with a proper ventilation system) by suspending them from the upper portions of the cabinet so that all surfaces will be exposed to the fumes.
2. Place two or three drops of liquid cyanoacrylate into a small porcelain dish and place the dish in the fuming cabinet.

3. Allow the items to be exposed to the fumes for at least 2 hours until whitish colored print pattern(s) appear on the object.
4. The developed print may be enhanced by dusting with regular or magnetic print powder after fuming. (Lee and Gaensslen 2001, pp. 117–118)

## Cyanoacrylate Fuming (Microburst Method)

Cyanoacrylate fuming is used to develop latent prints on nonporous specimens.

## Processing Procedure

Using the fuming chamber:

1. Place the aluminum dish on a heating surface and turn the heater to the highest setting.
2. When the dish is hot, place enough liquid cyanoacrylate to cover the bottom surface of the dish (approximately 3 g for a small chamber).
3. When the cyanoacrylate begins to fume at a steady pace, place the specimen(s) in the chamber and secure the chamber door.
4. Fume the specimen(s). Fuming time varies depending on the size of the chamber; however, in most instances, fuming times ranging from 30 seconds to 4 minutes are sufficient.
5. After the procedure is complete, remove the specimen(s) from the chamber to view for latent prints. If necessary, the fuming process can be repeated. If a humidified chamber is available, set the humidity between 70% and 80% for best results.

The accumulation of cyanoacrylate glue fumes on some parts of a firearm could have an unfavorable effect during a subsequent firearms examination. In those instances when a firearms examination is to be done or anticipated, each chamber opening (e.g., the cylinder of a revolver) and each barrel opening should be covered with a small piece of tape (just large enough to cover the opening) before fuming with glue. Ensure that the area to be covered by the tape is processed by other appropriate methods prior to covering. Remove the tape after the cyanoacrylate glue fuming process (Trozzi, Schwartz, and Hollars 2000, p. 21).

## Modification Accelerating Fuming Procedure

### Fume Circulation Procedure

To increase the surface contact, a circulation procedure may be used. This is done by following the above protocol, but a fan or small air-circulating pump is placed in the cabinet in order to circulate the fumes (Lee and Gaensslen 2001, pp. 118–119).

### Heat Acceleration Procedure

To increase the vapor release, a heating procedure may be used. This is done by following the general protocol, but in addition, a heating apparatus (light bulb, portable heater, hot plate, hair dryer, or alcohol lamp) may be placed so as to heat the porcelain dish. This will accelerate the polymerization process and increase monomer volatility. This causes vapors to release faster and in turn, development time will decrease (Lee and Gaensslen 2001, pp. 118–119).

### Chemical Acceleration Procedure

For this procedure, a clean cotton pad or ball or other absorbent material is placed in the dish. Two to three drops of liquid cyano-acrylate are placed on the material, followed by two or three drops of 0.5 N sodium hydroxide solution.[2] The moisture is then allowed to fume for 30 min to1 hour until a white print develops (Lee and Gaensslen 2001, pp. 118–119).

# Methods Enhancing Cyanoacrylate Fuming

### Cyanoacrylate Fluorescent Dye (RAM)

This formula is used to dye cyanoacrylate developed latent prints. These prints can then be better visualized by the use of a laser or alternate light source. This method is effective on all colors of non-porous surfaces. Additional formulas for dyes used to enhance cyanoacrylate developed latent prints can be found in later sections of this guide.

### Mixing Procedure

Two stock solutions must be mixed prior to formulating the RAM dye.

### Stock Solution 1 (Rhodamine 6G)

| | |
|---|---|
| Rhodamine 6G | 1 g |
| Methanol | 1000 mL |

Combine the ingredients and place on a stirring device until all the rhodamine 6G is thoroughly dissolved.

### Stock Solution 2 (MBD)

| | |
|---|---|
| MBD | 1 g |
| Acetone | 1000 mL |

---

[2] To prepare a 0.5 N sodium hydroxide solution, dissolve 2 g of solid NaOH in 100 mL of distilled water.

Combine the ingredients and place on a stirring device until all the MBD is thoroughly dissolved.

### Ardrox P133D

Ardrox is used undiluted directly from the container.

### RAM Working Solution

| | |
|---|---|
| Stock Solution 1 | 3 mL |
| Ardrox P133D | 2 mL |
| Stock Solution 2 | 7 mL |
| Methanol | 20 mL |
| Isopropanol | 10 mL |
| Acetonitrile | 8 mL |
| Petroleum Ether | 950 mL |

Combine the ingredients in the order listed. ***Do not place on a magnetic stirrer***.

### Processing Procedure

After a specimen has been processed with cyanoacrylate, RAM can be applied by spraying, dipping, or using a squirt bottle, followed by examination under a laser or alternate light source (Trozzi, Schwartz, and Hollars 2000, p. 19).

### MBD (Fluorescent Dye)

MBD is a fluorescent dye used to make cyanoacrylate developed latent prints more visible on various colored surfaces. A laser or alternate light source is used in conjunction with this process.

### Mixing Procedure

### Stock Solution

| | |
|---|---|
| MBD | 1 g |
| Acetone | 1000 mL |

Combine the ingredients and stir on a stirring device until all MBD is dissolved.

### Working Solution

| | |
|---|---|
| MBD Stock Solution | 10 mL |
| Methanol | 30 mL |
| Isopropanol | 10 mL |
| Petroleum Ether | 950 mL |

Combine the ingredients in the order listed. ***Do not place on a magnetic stirrer.***

### Procedure

1. Dip the specimen or use a squirt bottle to apply the solution after the cyanoacrylate fuming process.
2. Examine under a laser or alternate light source (Trozzi, Schwartz, and Hollars 2000, p. 52).

## MRM 10 (Fluorescent Dye)

MRM 10 is a fluorescent dye used to enhance cyanoacrylate developed latent prints on various colored nonporous surfaces. A laser or alternate light source is used in conjunction with this process.

### Mixing Procedures

Prior to mixing the MRM 10 cyanoacrylate dye solution, stock solutions A, B, and C must be prepared.

### Stock Solution A

| | |
|---|---|
| Rhodamine 6G | 1 g |
| Methanol | 1000 mL |

Combine the ingredients and place on a stirring device until all the rhodamine 6G is dissolved.

### Stock Solution B

| | |
|---|---|
| Maxillon Flavine 10GFF | 2 g |
| Methanol | 1000 mL |

Combine the ingredients and place on a stirring device to dissolve the maxillon flavine 10GFF. **Not all the maxillon flavine 10GFF will dissolve. There will be a settlement in the bottom of the storage bottle, but this will not affect the working solution.**

### Stock Solution C

| | |
|---|---|
| MBD | 1 g |
| Acetone | 1000 mL |

Combine the ingredients and place on a stirring device to dissolve the MBD.

## MRM 10 Working Solution

| | |
|---|---|
| Stock Solution A | 3 mL |
| Stock Solution B | 3 mL |
| Stock Solution C | 7 mL |
| Methanol | 20 mL |
| Isopropanol | 10 mL |
| Acetonitrile | 8 mL |
| Petroleum Ether | 950 mL |

Combine the ingredients in the order listed. ***Do not place on a stirring device***.

### Procedure

1. Dip, spray, or use a squirt bottle to apply the MRM 10 working solution. Leave on for approximately 30 to 90 seconds.
2. Apply the rinse.
3. Repeat to improve contrast.
4. Apply the final rinse of distilled water or tap water. (Trozzi, Schwartz, and Hollars 2000, p. 54)

## Ardrox (Fluorescent Dye)

This dye is used in conjunction with a long-wave ultraviolet light source.

### Working Solution

| | |
|---|---|
| Ardrox P133D | 2 mL |
| Acetone | 10 mL |
| Methanol | 25 mL |
| Isopropanol | 10 mL |
| Acetonitrile | 8 mL |
| Petroleum Ether | 945 mL |

Combine the ingredients in the order listed. ***Do not place on a magnetic stirrer***.

### Procedure

Apply by either dipping or using a squirt bottle (Trozzi, Schwartz, and Hollars 2000, p. 45).

## Rhodamine 6G (Fluorescent Dye)

Rhodamine 6G is a fluorescent dye used to make cyanoacrylate developed latent prints more visible on various colored surfaces.

A laser or alternate light source is used in conjunction with this process.

### Stock Solution

| | |
|---|---|
| Rhodamine 6G | 1 g |
| Methanol | 1000 mL |

Combine the ingredients and place on a stirring device until all the rhodamine 6G is dissolved.

### Working Solution

| | |
|---|---|
| Rhodamine 6G Stock Solution | 3 mL |
| Acetone | 15 mL |
| Acetonitrile | 10 mL |
| Methanol | 15 mL |
| Isopropanol | 32 mL |
| Petroleum Ether | 925 mL |

Combine the ingredients in the order listed. ***Do not place on a magnetic stirrer.***

### Procedure

1. Dip the specimen or use a squirt bottle to apply the rhodamine 6G working solution after the cyanoacrylate fuming process.
2. Examine under a laser or alternate light source (Trozzi, Schwartz, and Hollars 2000, p. 57).

### Safranin O (Fluorescent Dye)

Safranin O is a fluorescent dye used to develop or enhance cyanoacrylate developed latent prints. This dye is very effective at the low 500 nm region.

### Mixing Procedure

| | |
|---|---|
| Safranin O | 1 g |
| Methanol | 1000 mL |

Combine the ingredients and place on a stirring device for approximately 15 minutes.

### Procedure

1. Dip or spray the specimen or use a squirt bottle to apply the safranin O solution after the cyanoacrylate fuming process. (Excess solution may be removed using a methanol rinse.)

2. Let air dry or use a heat gun for drying.
3. Examine under a laser or alternate light source. (Trozzi, Schwartz, and Hollars 2000, p. 59)

### *Thenoyl Europium Chelate (Fluorescent Dye)*

Thenoyl europium chelate is a fluorescent dye used to stain cyano-acrylate developed latent prints. The dye can be viewed only under ultraviolet light.

### Stock Solution—Part A

| | |
|---|---|
| Thenoyltrifluoroacetone | 1 g |
| Methyl Ethyl Ketone | 200 mL |

### Stock Solution—Part B

| | |
|---|---|
| Europium Chloride Hexahydrate | 0.5 g |
| Distilled Water | 800 mL |

Combine solutions A and B. Place on a magnetic stirrer in a sealed container for 15 to 30 minutes. **The sealed container is necessary due to evaporation of the methyl ethyl ketone.**

### Working Solution

| | |
|---|---|
| Stock Solution | 100 mL |
| Methyl Ethyl Ketone | 180 mL |
| Distilled Water | 720 mL |

Combine the ingredients and place in a sealed container. Stir for ~15 minutes with stirrer.

### Procedure

### Submersion Method

1. Submerge the specimen in the working solution for approximately 2 minutes.
2. Let the specimen dry. Examine under long-wave ultraviolet light.

### Squirt Bottle Method

1. While viewing the specimen under long-wave ultraviolet light, apply the working solution with a squirt bottle. *Keep applying the working solution until maximum development occurs.*
2. If the working solution dye adheres to the background, a rinse consisting of 800 mL methanol and 200 mL distilled water can be applied. The rinse does not have to be mixed on a magnetic stirrer.

3. Submerge or use a squirt bottle to apply the rinse. (Trozzi, Schwartz, and Hollars 2000, pp. 60–61)

### DFO (1,8-Diazafluoren-9-One)

DFO reacts with the amino acids in perspiration. When this reaction is complete, the developed latent prints will fluoresce with the use of a laser or an alternate light source.

### DFO Stock Solution

| | |
|---|---|
| DFO | 1 g |
| Methanol | 200 mL |
| Ethyl Acetate | 200 mL |
| Glacial Acetic Acid | 40 mL |

Mix the above ingredients and stir with a stirring device until the DFO is dissolved (~20 min).

### Working Solution

Dilute the stock solution to 2 L with petroleum ether. This solution should be a clear gold color.

### Procedure

1. Dip or spray the object until covered with DFO.
2. Dry the object and place it in an oven, 100°C (212°F), for 20 minutes. If an oven is not available, a dry iron, such as a steam iron with the steam turned off, may be used. (Trozzi, Schwartz, and Hollars 2000, p. 24)

## Ninhydrin—Various Methods

### Ninhydrin

Ninhydrin is usually used to develop latent prints on porous surfaces. It reacts with the amino acids in perspiration, and thus print residue, giving a bluish-purple print.

Reagents: stock ninhydrin solution, working solution, filtered final solution.

### Ninhydrin Stock Solution

| | |
|---|---|
| Ninhydrin | 15 g |
| Glacial Acetic Acid | 30 mL |
| Absolute Ethanol | 60 mL |

## Working Solution

Dilute 3 mL of stock solution with 100 mL dry fluorisol.[3] Mix the stock solution with the dry Freon, stir well, and let stand for 20 minutes. Filter and store in dark bottle.

## Procedure

1. Fill the sprayer with the working solution and spray the surface the latent print is on. Spray from a distance of 6 inches.
2. Allow it to evaporate, then repeat.
3. After spraying, the surface may shortly be heated with an infrared lamp or steam iron. (Care must be taken not to overheat or touch the heat source to the object.) This step will accelerate print development.
4. If desired, step 3 may be omitted and the specimen may be left at room temperature until the print develops. (Doing this instead often yields more satisfactory results.)

When this reaction is complete, the developed latent prints will fluoresce with the use of a laser or an alternate light source (Lee and Gaensslen 2001, pp. 73–74)

### Ninhydrin (Acetone Base)

## Mixing Procedure

| | |
|---|---|
| Ninhydrin | 6 g |
| Acetone | 1000 mL |

The ninhydrin crystals will readily dissolve in acetone. Minimal stirring is required.

## Procedure

Spray, dip, or paint the specimen with the ninhydrin solution. Ninhydrin must be dried before any attempt is made to accelerate the development process. **Ninhydrin must be subjected to a humidified environment (e.g., a humidified chamber or an iron on the steam setting).** If a humidified chamber is available, set humidity between 60% and 70% for best results (Trozzi, Schwartz, and Hollars 2000, p. 56).

### Ninhydrin (Petroleum Ether Base)

Ninhydrin is used to develop latent prints on porous surfaces. Ninhydrin reacts with the amino acids present in perspiration.

---

[3] Fluorisol—(1,1,2-trifluorotrichloroethane)

## Mixing Procedure

| Ninhydrin | 5 g |
|---|---|
| Methanol | 30 mL |
| Isopropanol | 40 mL |
| Petroleum Ether | 930 mL |

The ninhydrin crystals are first dissolved in methanol on a stirring device. Then the isopropanol is added, followed by the petroleum ether.

## Procedure

The ninhydrin solution can be applied to a specimen by spraying, dipping, or painting. Once the solution has been applied, it must be dried before any attempt is made to accelerate the development process using a humidified environment (e.g., a humidified chamber or a steam iron). If a humidified chamber is available, set humidity between 60% and 70% for best results (Trozzi, Schwartz, and Hollars 2000, p. 33).

### Small Particle Reagent[4]

S.P.R. is a reagent used for processing latent prints on items that are wet when recovered. It is most often used where powders are ineffective. This reagent also works effectively on items that have been soaked in liquid accelerants. This technique requires a large work area that will be subject to messy conditions. The active ingredient, molybdenum disulfide, is applied by either spraying or dipping the item. S.P.R. can also be used as a post-cyanoacrylate process when dye stains are ineffective. Application of the reagent may be repeated to enhance any faintly developed ridge detail. The developed ridge detail may be lifted after being photographed (CBD-IAI, 2001–2002).

## Solution #1

| Choline Chloride | 4 g |
|---|---|
| Tergitol 7 | 8 ml |
| Distilled Water | 500 ml |

Stir.

## Solution #2

| Molybdenum Disulfide | 10 g |
|---|---|
| Solution #1 | 50 ml |

Stir.

---

[4] S.P.R. is less effective on items that have dried after being wet.

**Solution #3:**

Add 900 ml distilled water to solution #2.
Stir.

— or —

**Combine the following into a suspension:**

| | |
|---|---|
| Tergitol (detergent) | 0.4 ml |
| Molybdenum Disulfide | 5 g |
| Distilled Water | 50 ml |

**Tray Immersion Procedure (best method)**

1. Dip item in solution mixture and keep stationary for 1 minute.
2. Tray rinse excess reagent in tap water for 15 seconds.
3. Allow the item to dry at room temperature.
4. The dried print may be able to be lifted after photographing any developed detail.

**Squirt/Spray Procedure**

1. Shake well and apply reagent to item. Repeat for 1 minute.
2. Rinse under running tap water for 15 seconds.
3. Allow the item to dry at room temperature.
4. The dried print may be able to be lifted after photographing any developed detail. (CBD-IAI, 2001–2002)

## Collection and Preservation of Patent Fingerprints

Patent fingerprints are another form of fingerprints found at crime scenes. They are defined as prints that are visible when found. In some instances it may be necessary to take swabs of certain items to allow examination for DNA or biological fluids. This must be done before any prints are processed.

## Special Situations—Visualization/Lifting in Blood

### Amido Black (Methanol Base[5])

The amido black process consists of two solutions, a developer and a rinse, and a final rinse of distilled water.

---

[5] Caution must be exercised when applying the methanol-based formula to painted surfaces. This formula may destroy the latent print(s) as well as the surface beneath the latent print(s). All blood must be dried prior to application. Cyanoacrylate fuming may be detrimental to this process.

## Mixing Procedure

### Developer Solution

| | |
|---|---|
| Naphthol Blue Black | 2 g |
| Glacial Acetic Acid | 100 mL |
| Methanol | 900 mL |

Combine the ingredients. Mix using a stirring device until all the naphthol blue black is dissolved, approximately 30 minutes.

### Rinse Solution

| | |
|---|---|
| Glacial Acetic Acid | 100 mL |
| Methanol | 900 mL |

Combine the ingredients.

### Procedure

1. Dip, spray, or use a squirt bottle to add the developer to the specimen. Let set for approximately 30 seconds to 1 minute.
2. Apply the rinse.
3. Repeat to improve contrast.
4. Apply the final rinse of distilled or tap water.
5. Dry the specimen(s). (Trozzi, Schwartz, and Hollars 2000, p. 14)

## *Amido Black (Water Base–Fischer 98)*

### Mixing Procedure

| | |
|---|---|
| Distilled Water | 500 mL |
| 5 Sulfosalicylic Acid | 20 g |
| Naphthol Blue Black | 3 g |
| Sodium Carbonate | 3 g |
| Formic Acid | 50 mL |
| Glacial Acetic Acid | 50 mL |
| Kodak Photo-Flo™ 600 Solution | 12.5 mL |

Prepare by mixing all ingredients, in order listed, with a stirring device.

Dilute this mixture to 1 L using distilled water. Allow the mixture to stand for several days prior to use for best results, but the mixture may be used immediately if needed.

### Procedure

1. Dip specimen or use a squirt bottle to apply the amido black to the specimen(s).
2. Leave the solution on for 3 to 5 minutes.
3. Rinse using tap water.
4. Repeat for the desired contrast. (Trozzi, Schwartz, and Hollars 2000, p. 16)

### *Coomassie Brilliant Blue*

Coomassie brilliant blue is used to develop latent prints and enhance visible prints deposited in blood.

### Developer Solution

| | |
|---|---|
| Coomassie Brilliant Blue R | 0.96 g |
| Glacial Acetic Acid | 84 mL |
| Methanol | 410 mL |
| Distilled Water | 410 mL |

Combine the ingredients and place on a stirring device until all the Coomassie brilliant blue is dissolved (~ 30 min).

### Rinse Solution

| | |
|---|---|
| Glacial Acetic Acid | 100 mL |
| Methanol | 450 mL |
| Distilled Water | 450 mL |

Combine the ingredients.

### Procedure

1. Dip, spray, or use a squirt bottle to apply the developer solution. Leave on for approximately 30 to 90 seconds.
2. Apply the rinse.
3. Repeat to improve contrast.
4. Apply the final rinse of distilled water or tap water. (Trozzi, Schwartz, and Hollars 2000, p. 47)

### *DAB [6] (Diaminobenzidine)*

DAB can be applied by two methods—the submersion method and the tissue method.

### Mixing Procedure

The DAB process consists of four solutions—A, B, C, and a developer.

### Solution A (Fixer)

| | |
|---|---|
| 5-Sulfosalicylic Acid | 20 g |
| Distilled Water | 1000 mL |

Combine the ingredients and place on a stirring device until thoroughly dissolved.

---

[6] Cyanoacrylate fuming can be detrimental to all blood DAB processing. DAB processing must be completed before processing with cyanoacrylate.

### Solution B (Buffer)

| | |
|---|---|
| 1M Phosphate Buffer Solution (pH 7.4) | 100 mL |
| Distilled Water | 800 mL |

Combine the ingredients.

### Solution C (DAB)

| | |
|---|---|
| 3, 3′-Diaminobenzidine Tetrahydrochloride | 1 g |
| Distilled Water | 100 mL |

Combine the ingredients and mix thoroughly.

### Developer Solution

| | |
|---|---|
| Solution B | 180 mL |
| Solution C | 20 mL |
| Hydrogen Peroxide 30% | 1 mL |

Combine the ingredients and mix thoroughly.

### Submersion Method

This method consists of four steps using four trays.

**Step 1—Tray 1** This tray contains the **fixer solution** (Solution A). Submerge the specimen(s) in this solution for approximately 3 to 5 minutes.

**Step 2—Tray 2** This tray contains **distilled water** for rinsing the specimen(s). Submerge the specimen(s) in the water for 30 seconds to 1 minute.

**Step 3—Tray 3** This tray contains the **developer solution**. Submerge the specimen(s) in this solution for 5 minutes for maximum development. The specimen(s) may be removed prior to 5 minutes if maximum development or contrast has been achieved.

**Step 4—Tray 4** This tray contains another **distilled water rinse**. Submerge the specimen(s) in the water to stop the developer solution from overdeveloping the print(s).

The specimen(s) can now be air dried or dried with heat (e.g., a heat gun).

### Tissue Method

Tissues are placed over the area to be processed and solutions are applied using a squirt bottle or a sprayer. The tissues used for this process must be durable enough to be placed and picked up while wet, without disintegrating. Perfumed tissues should not be used because the chemicals can interfere with the development process. Unscented white facial or hand tissues and thin paper towels are acceptable.

**Step 1—Bottle 1** This bottle contains the **fixer solution** (Solution A). Squirt this solution onto a tissue that has been placed on the area to be examined. The tissue adheres to the area because it is wet from the fixer. The tissue should be kept wet for 3 to 5 minutes.

**Step 2—Bottle 2** This bottle contains **distilled water**. Remove the tissue, then squirt the water on the processed area for 30 seconds to 1 minute.

**Step 3—Bottle 3** This bottle contains the **developer solution**. At this point, it is very important that a new tissue is used. After the new tissue is placed on the area to be examined, the developer solution is applied to the tissue. The tissue must be kept wet at all times and maintained on the area for 5 minutes. This time period may be less if maximum development or contrast has been achieved.

**Step 4—Bottle 2** Repeat Step 2.

### Storage

*Solution A*—dark bottle stored at room temperature
*Solution B*—dark bottle stored at room temperature
*Solution C*—plastic bottle or container that can withstand extreme cold, stored in a freezer. Hydrogen peroxide (30%) must be stored in a refrigerator (Trozzi, Schwartz, and Hollars 2000, pp. 21–23).

### LCV (Leucocrystal Violet)

LCV is used to enhance visual prints and develop latent prints deposited in blood. **Warning: Cyanoacrylate fuming may be detrimental to this process.**

### Mixing Procedure

| | |
|---|---|
| Hydrogen Peroxide 3% | 1000 mL |
| 5-Sulfosalicylic Acid | 20 g |
| Sodium Acetate | 7.4 g |
| LCV | 2 g |

Combine ingredients in the order listed and place on a stirring device for approximately 30 minutes.

### Procedure

1. Spray the finest mist possible (because excess application may cause overdevelopment or running of the bloody print).
2. Development will occur within 30 seconds.
3. Blot the area with a tissue or paper towel.
4. When the area is dry, the process can be repeated to possibly improve contrast.
5. When using the LCV process in direct sunlight, any developed print should be photographed as soon as possible

because photo-ionization may occur, resulting in unwanted background development. (Trozzi, Schwartz, and Hollars 2000, p. 31)

### Crowle's Double Stain

Crowle's double stain is used for visualization of prints in blood.

### Developer Solution

| | |
|---|---|
| Crocein Scarlet 7B | 2.5 g |
| Coomassie Brilliant Blue R | 150 mg |
| Glacial Acetic Acid | 50 mL |
| Trichloroacetic Acid | 30 mL |

Combine the ingredients, then dilute to 1 L using distilled water. Place on a stirring device for approximately 30 minutes until all the Crocein scarlet 7B and Coomassie brilliant blue R are dissolved.

### Rinse Solution

| | |
|---|---|
| Glacial Acetic Acid | 30 mL |
| Distilled Water | 970 mL |

Combine the ingredients.

### Procedure

1. Dip, spray, or use a squirt bottle to apply the developer solution. Leave on for approximately 30 to 90 seconds.
2. Apply the rinse.
3. Repeat to improve contrast.
4. Apply the final rinse of distilled water or tap water. (Trozzi, Schwartz, and Hollars 2000, p. 49)

## Special Situations—Visualization/Lifting on Tape

Lifting prints from both the adhesive and nonadhesive side of tape and labels is sometimes required. The most commonly used methods are listed as follows.

### Alternate Black Powder

Alternate black powder is used to process the sticky side of adhesive tapes and labels for latent prints.

### Mixing Procedure

| | |
|---|---|
| Lightning® Black Powder | 1 tsp |
| Liqui-Drox™ Solution (diluted 50:50 with water) | 40 drops |

Combine the Lightning black powder and Liqui-Drox™ solution in a petri or shallow dish and stir until the solution has a shaving cream consistency.

### Procedure

1. Paint the solution on the adhesive surface of the tape with a camel-hair or small brush. Allow to set for 30 to 60 seconds.
2. Rinse off the solution with a slow stream of cold tap water. Allow to dry.
3. Repeat the procedure if necessary. (Trozzi, Schwartz, and Hollars 2000, p. 10)

### Ash Gray Powder

Ash gray powder is used to process the sticky side of adhesive tapes and labels for latent prints. This method is particularly useful on dark-colored and black tape.

### Mixing Procedure

| | |
|---|---|
| Ash Gray Powder | 1 tsp |
| Photo-Flo™ 200 or Photo-Flo™ | 600 Solution |

Place the ash gray powder in a petri or shallow dish. Add enough Photo-Flo™ solution to the powder to make a solution the consistency of thin paint when mixed.

### Procedure

1. Paint the solution on the adhesive surface of the tape with a camel-hair or small brush. Allow to set for 30 to 60 seconds.
2. Rinse off the solution with a slow stream of cold tap water. Allow to dry.
3. Repeat the procedure if necessary. (Trozzi, Schwartz, and Hollars 2000, p. 10)

### Gentian Violet

Gentian violet is used to develop latent prints on the adhesive side of tape. *Water-soluble, adhesive-type tapes should not be processed by this method.*

### Mixing Procedure

| | |
|---|---|
| Gentian Violet Crystals or | 1 g |
| Gentian Violet Solution | 1 ml |
| Distilled Water | 1000 mL |

Combine the ingredients and place on a stirring device for approximately 25 minutes. *The gentian violet solution can be reused.*

## Procedure

1. Dip the specimen(s) in the gentian violet solution for approximately 1 to 2 minutes.
2. Rinse with cold tap water for approximately 30 seconds.

Print may be viewed using light source between 505–570 nm using red goggles (Trozzi, Schwartz, and Hollars 2000, p. 12).

### Sticky-Side Powder

Sticky-side powder is used to process the sticky side of adhesive tapes and labels for latent prints.

### Mixing Procedure

| | |
|---|---|
| Sticky-Side Powder | 1 tsp |
| Photo-Flo™ | 100 Solution |

*Make 100 solution by mixing Photo-Flo 200 1:1 with distilled water.* Place the sticky-side powder in a petri or shallow dish. Add enough Photo-Flo™ 100 solution to the powder to make a mixture the consistency of thin paint when stirred.

### Procedure

1. Paint the solution on the adhesive surface of the tape with a camel-hair or small brush. Allow to set for 30 to 60 seconds.
2. Rinse off the solution with a slow stream of cold tap water. Allow to dry.
3. Repeat the procedure if necessary. (Trozzi, Schwartz, and Hollars 2000, p. 10)

### Liqui-Drox™

Liqui-Drox™ is a fluorescent dye used to develop latent prints on the adhesive and nonadhesive sides of dark-colored tape.

### Mixing Procedure

| | |
|---|---|
| Ardrox P133D | 200 mL |
| Liqui-Drox™ | 400 mL |
| Distilled Water | 400 mL |

Combine the ingredients and stir thoroughly. The solution should be thick and have a milky yellow color. **The Liqui-Drox™ solution will become clear with time and should not be used in this condition. Stir to return the milky color to the solution and use as normal.**

**Procedure**

1. Apply the Liqui-Drox™ solution with a small brush to both sides of the tape, provided the nonadhesive side of the tape has been cyanoacrylate fumed. Brush until a lather is produced.
2. Allow the solution to sit on the tape for about 10 seconds.
3. Rinse the tape under a stream of water until Liqui-Drox™ is no longer visible. Allow the tape to dry.
4. View the tape under a long-wave ultraviolet light.
5. Photograph promptly because the ridge detail begins to fade within 12 hours. Do not leave the specimen under the ultraviolet light for extended periods of time because this will cause the latent print to fade. (Trozzi, Schwartz, and Hollars 2000, p. 51)

## Special Situations—Visualization/Lifting on Currency

### *Physical Developer (PD)*

Physical developer (PD) is used to develop latent prints on porous surfaces and on certain nonporous surfaces. Physical developer has also been found to be highly effective in developing latent prints on paper currency. Physical developer is normally applied after the DFO and/or ninhydrin methods. Sodium hypochlorite can also be used in conjunction with physical developer. The sodium hypochlorite solution darkens the latent print(s) developed with physical developer, lightens the background, and removes any ninhydrin stains that may still be present on the specimen(s). This process is especially effective on paper bags and paper currency. Mixing and processing procedures for sodium hypochlorite follow those listed for physical developer.

Stains on blueprints, photographs, or photostats caused by physical developer treatment cannot be removed without defacing the specimens. This process cannot be used in conjunction with the silver nitrate method. If the PD process is used, it will negate the silver nitrate process.

**Mixing Procedure**

Physical developer is mixed in four solutions. (Each must be placed on a stirring device until all the chemicals are thoroughly dissolved.)

**Solution 1 (Maleic Acid)**

| | |
|---|---|
| Maleic Acid | 25 g |
| Distilled Water | 1000 mL |

### Solution 2 (Redox)

| | |
|---|---|
| Ferric Nitrate | 30 g |
| Ferrous Ammonium Sulfate | 80 g |
| Citric Acid | 20 g |
| Distilled Water | 1000 mL |

### Solution 3 (Detergent)

| | |
|---|---|
| n-Dodecylamine Acetate | 3 g |
| Synperonic-N | 4 g |
| Distilled Water | 1000 mL |

### Solution 4 (Silver Nitrate)

| | |
|---|---|
| Silver Nitrate | 200 g |
| Distilled Water | 1000 mL |

### Procedure

#### Tray 1—Solution 1 (Maleic Acid)

Submerge specimen(s) in Solution 1. Leave in this solution for 5 minutes. If a specimen begins to emit bubbles, it must be submerged in the solution until the bubbling action ceases.

#### Tray 2—Solution 2 (Redox Working Solution)

| | |
|---|---|
| Solution 2 | 1000 mL |
| Solution 3 | 40 mL |
| Solution 4 | 50 mL |

1. Combine solutions in the order listed. (Place Solution 2 in a beaker on a stirring device. Add Solutions 3 and 4 and stir for 3 to 5 minutes.)
2. Place in Tray 2 and place on an orbital shaker[7] set for a gentle rocking motion of the redox working solution to assist the development process.
3. Submerge the specimen(s) for 5 to 15 minutes. The amount of time will depend on the number of specimens per tray. Generally, the more specimens in the tray, the longer the reaction time will be.

*Approximately 15 check-sized specimens can normally be processed with 1 L of redox working solution.*

---

[7] If an orbital shaker is not available, rocking Tray 2 back and forth manually can also be effective.

### Tray 3—Water Rinse

4. Remove from the redox working solution and rinse with water. (If this is not done the specimen will become brittle and may be easily damaged or destroyed.)
5. Remove from the rinse and either heat or air dry.

## *Sodium Hypochlorite Mixing Procedure*

### Working Solution

| | |
|---|---|
| Sodium Hypochlorite | 500 mL |
| Distilled Water | 500 mL |

### Procedure

1. After it has been processed and rinsed with PD, dip the specimen in the sodium hypochlorite solution for approximately 15 seconds.
2. Rinse again with water. (If the specimen is not thoroughly rinsed, deterioration of the specimen may occur.) (Trozzi, Schwartz, and Hollars 2000, p. 34)

# Special Situations—Visualization/Lifting from Oily/Greasy Surfaces

## *Sudan Black*

Sudan black is a dye that stains sebaceous perspiration to produce a blue-black image. This method is useful on surfaces contaminated with foodstuff, oils, and other greasy substances.

### Mixing Procedure

| | |
|---|---|
| Sudan Black | 15 g |
| Ethanol | 1000 mL |
| Distilled Water | 500 mL |

Combine the Sudan black and the ethanol and stir. Then add the distilled water and stir to obtain the working solution. **Some of the Sudan black will not be dissolved.**

### Procedure

1. Shake working solution and pour a sufficient amount into a glass tray.
2. Immerse the specimen(s) in the solution for approximately 2 minutes.
3. Remove the specimen(s)
4. Rinse with tap water, and let dry. (Trozzi, Schwartz, and Hollars 2000, p. 40)

## Special Situations—Visualization/Lifting from Magazines/Photos

### *Vacuum Metal Deposition (VMD)*

Vacuum metal deposition is used to develop latent prints on non-porous specimens and some semiporous specimens (e.g., magazine pages and photographs). ***Vacuum metal deposition developed prints are fragile. Extreme caution should be exercised when handling and photographing these specimens.*** These procedures are for a specific vacuum metal deposition chamber size. Various styles and sizes may require different procedures.

### Procedure

1. Place or suspend the specimen from the interior rack and secure the specimen to the rack with magnetic clips. A control card or test sample should also be placed on the interior rack. If the specimen needs to be rotated, remove the rotation probe and place in a plastic holder.
2. Place gold in the appropriate boats, using all six boats if the specimen needs to be rotated, but only the second, fourth, and sixth if processing only one side. Be sure to check the boats for stress cracks and replace if needed. Approximately 0.04 g of the gold will be thermalized for each sequence.
3. Check the zinc pots for defects, replace if necessary, and check for and add zinc as needed.
4. Pump the chamber down to the proper operating pressure range: 10-4 torr. The vacuum ready light on the instrument display panel will indicate when this is done (approximately 10 minutes).
5. Once the desired vacuum is obtained, set the current switch to gold and adjust the power control knob to 195. Heat until all gold in the three boats has been thermalized (approximately 10 seconds). (This should be observed through one of the viewing ports while wearing welder's goggles.)
6. Turn the current switch off for approximately 15 seconds.
7. Set the current switch to zinc and adjust the power control knob to 52. Allow 1 minute to 1 minute 45 seconds for the zinc to thermalize. Observe the control sample through the viewing port for the correct zinc development.
8. Repeat steps 5 through 7 after setting the rotate switch, if the specimen needs to be rotated.
9. Wait approximately 30 seconds and vent the chamber. (Trozzi, Schwartz, and Hollars 2000, p. 41)

## Special Situations—Visualization/Lifting on Painted Surfaces

### *Amido Black (Water Base)*

The amido black water-based formula is used in place of the methanol-based formula when there is a question about or a problem with a painted surface. *If it is a bloody print, all blood must be thoroughly dried before applying this formula. Cyanoacrylate fuming may be detrimental to the amido black water-based formula.*

### Mixing Procedure

### Citric Acid Stock Solution (also rinse solution)

| | |
|---|---|
| Citric Acid | 38 g |
| Distilled Water | 2000 mL |

Combine the ingredients and place on a stirring device until citric acid is completely dissolved.

### Developer Solution

| | |
|---|---|
| Citric Acid Stock Solution | 1000 mL |
| Naphthol Blue Black | 2 g |
| Kodak Photo-Flo™ 600 Solution | 2 mL |

Combine the ingredients and place on a stirring device.

### Procedure

1. Dip, spray, or use a squirt bottle to apply the developer solution. Leave on for approximately 30 seconds to 1 minute.
2. Apply the rinse.
3. Repeat to improve contrast.
4. Apply the final rinse of distilled water or tap water, then dry the specimen. (Trozzi, Schwartz, and Hollars 2000, p. 43)

## Special Situations—Visualization/Lifting on Human Skin

Many procedures have been looked at and tested for the recovery of latent prints on skin. Those shown to be somewhat successful include iodine-silver plate transfer, cyanoacrylate fuming, Mars red fluorescent powder dusting, and staining with Rhodamine 6G followed by a laser examination. The method presented here is a combination of the previous methods and those taken from Lee and Gaensslen (2001).

### Procedure

1. Place a suitable tank, box, tent, or casket over the cadaver.
2. Put approximately 0.5 to 1.0 g Super Glue into the fuming chamber.
3. Place 500 mL hot water into a beaker and put this in the fuming chamber to increase humidity.
4. Fume the body for approximately 30 minutes to 1 hour.
5. Prepare the Rhodamine 6G magnetic powder
   a. Dissolve 0.1 g Rhodamine 6G in 50 mL methanol.
   b. Add 100 g black magnetic powder to the rhodamine solution.
   c. Heat the mixture, stirring constantly, until dried.
   d. Grind the dried mixture to fine powder.
6. Dust the body with the rhodamine-coated magnetic powder.
7. Examine the dusted area under laser light or any other light sources.
8. Photograph the developed latent print(s).

# Conclusion

### *Analysis and Identification of Impression/Imprint Evidence*

After developing the latent print, it needs to be determined whether it is suitable enough for identifying a person. The ridge detail needs to be satisfactory enough in quantity and quality in order to do a comparison with a known print. Once this determination is made, it is compared to known fingerprint cards. This is usually done with a computer system.

Fingerprint-based identification computer systems have been tremendously successful in forensic science applications. One computer system used for identifying latent fingerprints is called the automated fingerprint identification system (AFIS). It is a computerized database comprised of fingerprint images, fingerprint classification details, and full 10-print fingerprint records. A processed latent fingerprint is scanned onto the AFIS computer, and the fingerprint is enhanced using contrast and brightness. AFIS searches large files for the presence of a 10-print card taken from an individual and also searches large files for single prints that were most likely developed latent prints from crime scenes. This search specifically consists of comparing the minutiae detail of the unknown print to the known prints in the database. It is important to point out that AFIS never makes identification, but only lists possible matches that a fingerprint examiner would use to compare to the unknown print (Ridges and Furrows).

There are some disadvantages of this system, however. There are at least four different types of AFIS systems made by different commercial vendors, and therefore, they are not compatible with each other. One set of prints may be found in one system, but not found in another. A different AFIS computer system is called the Integrated Automated Fingerprint Identification System (IAFIS), which is created and controlled through the Federal Bureau of Investigation (FBI). It is a national criminal database containing all of the 10-print cards the FBI receives from across the country; therefore, it has been a very successful tool in identifying latent fingerprints (James and Norby 2005).

David Ashbaugh of the Royal Canadian Mounted Police (R.C.M.P.) described the scientific methodology of identifying a fingerprint as "A.C.E.V.": "analysis," "comparison," "evaluation," and "verification" from his book, *Quantitative-Qualitative Friction Ridge Analysis: An Introduction to Basic and Advanced Ridgeology*. The analysis step of the process consists of searching the print from the bottom to the top to ascertain if any distortion or color reversals could have occurred during the processing and determining the correct orientation of the print. The next step is comparing the unknown latent print with a known print. Comparison is made up of several levels. In level I, the overall ridge and pattern flow is examined. Next, the minutiae are compared in a point-by-point fashion in level II. Level III includes looking at the size and shape of edge features, as well as locations, numbers, pore shape, and relationships. If there are any unexplainable differences between the latent and the known print, then the known is automatically excluded as being the source of the latent. Evaluation occurs next by Ashbaugh's methodology. If there are enough details that are unique, and if every comparable feature between the known and latent prints is consistent, then the examiner can make identification. There is not a standard rule for a set number of points of identification, but a minimum of 10 to 12 points are commonly used. After the identification occurs, it needs to be verified by peer review by one or more latent fingerprint examiners. (Ashbaugh 1999; James and Norby 2005)

## Summary

Fingerprints are one of the oldest and most used types of physical evidence in crime scene investigations, and therefore, fingerprint examiners are an important part of the forensic science field. There is an extensive training period that fingerprint examiners must accomplish before becoming an independent specialist. The International Association for Identification (IAI) offers a certification program for latent fingerprint examiners, and there seems to be a trend for employers to require this certification prior to employment (James and Norby 2005).

# References

ASHBAUGH, D. R. 1999. *Quantitative-qualitative friction ridge analysis: An introduction to basic and advanced ridgeology.* Boca Raton, FL: CRC Press.

CBD-IAI. 2001–2002. *Latent fingerprint processing techniques: Selection & sequencing guide.* Retrieved September 26, 2005, from http://www.cbdiai.org/Reagents/main.html.

Federal Bureau of Investigation 1998. *The science of fingerprints: Classification and uses.* Washington, DC: U.S. Government Printing Office.

HENRY, E. R. 1913. *Classification and uses of finger prints.* London: HM Stationery Office.

JAMES, S. H., and J. J. NORBY (Eds.). 2005. *Forensic science: An introduction to scientific and investigative techniques* (2nd ed.). Boca Raton, FL: CRC Press.

LEE, H. C., and R. E. GAENSSLEN. 2001. Methods of latent fingerprint development. In H. Lee, and R. Gaensslen (Eds.), *Advances in fingerprint technology* (2nd ed., pp. 105–176). Boca Raton, FL: CRC Press.

MOENSSENS, A. A., F. E. INBAU, and J. E. STARRS. 1986. *Scientific evidence in criminal cases* (3rd ed.). Mineola, NY: Foundation Press.

RIDGES and FURROWS. (n.d.). *Automated fingerprint identification system (AFIS).* Retrieved November 3, 2005, from http://www.ridgesandfurrows.homestead.com/afispage.html.

RUSLANDER, H. W. 2001. *Searching and examining a major case crime scene.* Retrieved October 23, 2005, from http://www.crime-scene-investigator.net/searchingandexamining.html.

TROZZI, T. A., R. L. SCHWARTZ, and M. L. HOLLARS 2000. *Processing guide for developing latent fingerprints.* Retrieved September 9, 2005, from http://www.fbi.gov/hq/lab/fsc/backissu/jan2001/lpu.pdf.

# 2

# Footwear Impressions

*Amy Carlson and Jamie Lee*

## Introduction

The Edmond Locard Exchange principle states that every time one thing comes into contact with something else it takes something or leaves a portion of itself behind (Fisher, Svensson, and Wendel 1981). The surface of the ground is soft, so when a person takes a step they exert pressure which leaves an impression in the ground and causes deformation of the substrate. This can result in the material or residue being stepped in to transfer onto the shoe (Bodziak 2000, p. 8).

Sand, snow, mud, and blood are just some examples of different materials that can be transferred onto a variety of surfaces. Footwear can leave two forms of impression evidence, two-dimensional and three-dimensional. Two-dimensional footwear impressions do not have any depth and the residue that is stepped in is deposited on hard surfaces. These types of surfaces include tile floors, hardwood flooring, and furniture. Three-dimensional footwear impressions exhibit length, width, and depth and are found outdoors in snow, sand, and soil. Depending on the texture and composition of the substrate, the degree of detail will vary greatly (Bodziak 2000, p. 59).

When first encountering a two-dimensional footwear impression, electrostatic lifting should be used for clean surfaces. This technique does not harm the impression; if it is of a dry origin impression, the substance will transfer onto a black lifting film. If the impression does not lift using the electrostatic method, then the impression is of a wet origin. Black fingerprint powder along with a gelatin or adhesive lifter can be used to enhance an impression of wet origin. The color of the gelatin or adhesive lifters should contrast with the fingerprint powder. Gelatin and adhesive lifters are not the same. Gelatin is thicker, being composed of a cloth or vinyl backing and is covered with a thick layer of gelatin. Adhesive lifters consist of a plastic or paper backing coated with a high quality adhesive. Gelatin lifters are preferred as they have less sticky tack and can be used on nonporous and porous surfaces for the lifting of both original and dusted powder impressions (Bodziak 2000, pp. 115–120).

To cast three-dimensional impressions, plaster of Paris has been traditionally used; however, this form of casting is a messy, time-consuming procedure. The disadvantage is that plaster of Paris does not show much of the fine detail in the impressions because it is not a very hard form of gypsum. A new casting material that has been developed, which is a harder form of gypsum, is called *dental stone*. Dental stone provides better detail and dries quicker than plaster of Paris. Another method for casting impressions in snow is using a red aerosol spray called Snow Print Wax©; this causes a waxy mold to develop, thus preserving the detail in the snow impression. The wax shell can be filled with dental stone to provide stability when this shell is lifted from the ground. Sometimes, impressions are found in standing water. This type of impression must first have a full casting frame surrounding the footprint and then can be cast using dental stone (Bodziak 2000, pp. 65–69, 84–88).

Photography of the footwear impressions as well as documenting and sketching of the crime scene should be done before any lifting or casting procedures are performed. When photographing, two types of pictures should be taken: overall and examination quality photographs. The overall photograph should document the location of the footwear impression and the orientation of the surroundings. The examination quality photographs should be directly over the impression so that the investigator can have good visual detail (Bodziak 2000).

Evidence from footwear impressions can provide information that assists the investigation of a crime scene. Types of information that can be collected from shoe impressions are: identification of footwear, location of impressions, rebuttal or confirmation of suspects' alibis, determination of shoe brand, linking crime scenes, determination of shoe size, association with other evidence, and gait characteristics. Elimination, or narrowing down the suspect's shoe impressions, can determine whether or not the impressions are exculpatory evidence. It is significant if other individuals' shoes are located at a crime scene that had no authority to be there or if there are multiple shoe impressions which are indicative of many perpetrators committing the crime. Criminals can be tracked back to the scene of a crime by following a perpetrator's path of entry or exit, which gives insight into the location of the crime (Bodziak 2005, pp. 362–364).

The different types of information that can be collected from shoe impressions are based on the nature of class and individual characteristics of the shoe. Class characteristics focus on the size, style, shape, and pattern design of the shoe. The impression can be identified by the tread design on the outsole (bottom) of the shoe. Different tread designs are placed on the sole of the shoe from different manufacturers such as Nike, Adidas, Reebok, and so on. The treads function in gripping and traction between the individual and the surface the shoe comes in contact with. Also, the treads of shoes have different pattern designs which can identify the manufacturer. These designs are mesh, studs, quadrangular shape, and hollowed spaces (Astikainen and Mikkonen 1994).

In addition to looking for class characteristics, individual characteristics can be identified on the sole of the shoe. When a shoe is worn, subtle changes occur when it comes in contact with the ground causing other types of damage or injury to the sole. The abuse of the shoe is specific to the individual shoe. Different markings, cuts, and nicks on the sole of the shoe can distinguish between the many models of the same style shoe that a manufacturer produces. Some people walk pigeon toed (toed in) or toed out causing the sole to wear down more on the inside of the shoe or the outside of the shoe. Also, different terrains or environments can cause the sole to wear down in a unique way.

## Collection and Preservation of Shoe Impressions

### Documentation of Shoe Imprint Evidence

There are two common methods of documenting shoe imprint evidence: photography and sketching. Photography is very important because it allows the preservation and examination of evidence in its most unaltered form. Also, it is highly beneficial during documentation of a crime scene to photograph the location of other evidence in relation to the footwear impressions. Sketching allows for the exact dimensions of the crime scene to be displayed and the distance from the evidence to major objects to be known.

The first type of photographs taken at the scene should be a panoramic view of the entire area. Before taking the quality photographs of each individual shoe impression that will later be used for examination purposes, an overall photograph should be taken showing the scene and all the impressions. Some medium range and close range photographs should also be taken. After numbered evidence markers are placed next to each impression, overall photographs, mid-range photos, and close-up views of the scene should be reshot. Next, quality photographs of each impression should be taken so that they can be used for examination purposes. Generally, the cameras used for examination quality photographs are 4 × 5-in. or 35-mm. Although 4 × 5-in. cameras are typically better due to the larger size of the negatives, 35-mm cameras are most often used because they are less expensive. The first examination-style photograph should have the evidence number within the frame of the photo. The rest of the photos should be close-up, high quality, and have a measuring scale adjacent to the impression. The frame of each photograph should be completely filled with the impression, the scale, and the label (Hilderbrand 1999). The label should be a number that can later be referenced to a description and location of the print.

For three-dimensional impressions, the camera should be mounted on a tripod so that the camera is parallel with the ground and ninety degrees above the print. The flash should be placed at a 45° angle from the print and should be rotated and shot from at least three different positions. This will cause a lighting contrast so that more detail can be seen in the photos. If the impression is in direct sunlight, the print must be shadowed so that the flash method can be utilized (Hilderbrand 1999).

For two-dimensional impressions, the camera should be mounted in the same manner as with three-dimensional prints. The flash, however, should be placed close to the ground at least three or four feet away from the impression so that the light grazes the surface of the print (Hilderbrand 1999). This way the oblique light will reflect off the dust or other residue creating an examination-quality photograph. If the impression is on a light-colored surface, such as snow, the impression should be rephotographed after the print has been highlighted with either gray or black spray paint, fingerprint powder, or with Snow Print Wax©. When highlighting an impression with spray paint, the can should be placed about two feet away from the print. In this way, the force of the spray does not obliterate the impression.

The second method of documenting shoe print evidence is to sketch the scene, the location of the evidence, and the footwear impression itself. Usually crime scene sketches are done from an overhead view and measurements are taken from different permanent points, such as walls or corners, to the locations of each piece of evidence. The scene should be described or documented thoroughly including the location of major structures, points of entry, clothing, furniture, and weapons present.

### Collection of Residue Imprint Evidence

There are several different lifting methods employed to collect two-dimensional imprint evidence. Lifting allows for a two-dimensional impression to be transferred from its original location to a transportable surface for examination. The determination of which method to employ is based upon the condition and location of the print. Some of the variables that are important in determining which method to use are: the surface features (porous, nonporous, wet, dirty, etc.), the type of residue that the print is composed of, the color of the impression and the surface it is on, and the amount of humidity or moisture in the area that may affect electrostatic lifting. It is important to remember that lifting procedures result in a reversed image of the original print. The three most commonly used methods for lifting two-dimensional impressions are adhesive lifts, gelatin lifts, and the electrostatic dust lifter.

The first lifting method involves using adhesive paper. Adhesive footwear lifting materials are best when used on nonporous surfaces. Adhesive lifts come in a variety of colors and usually have a plastic or paper backing. Oftentimes before lifting a print using adhesive paper, the print is highlighted with fingerprint powder to provide greater contrast. Once the adhesive paper has been placed on the print, the paper is carefully lifted and the impression is transferred to the paper. After the impression is transferred to the sticky side of the adhesive lift, the paper can be treated with a stain. Crystal violet can be used to highlight the print for photography (Bodziak 2000). As shown in Figure 2.1, photos taken of the adhesive lift without any dye or fingerprint powder will result in poor resolution.

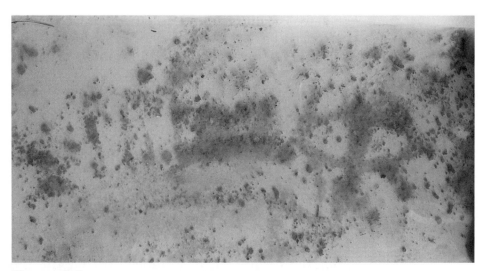

**Figure 2.1** Adhesive Lift without Dye or Fingerprint Powder

The second method involves using a gelatin lift. Gelatin lifts are thick and usually have a cloth or vinyl backing. Black gelatin lifts provide excellent contrast with light-colored dust and other residues. There are also white-colored gelatin lifts which can be used with black or fluorescent fingerprint powders. Another benefit of the gelatin lift is that they can be used on both porous and non-porous surfaces. Some disadvantages, however, are that they are capable of drying out over time and may lose their adhesive properties. They are also prone to damage in high heat conditions. Also, no dye can be used on the gelatin lifter (Bodziak 2000).

A third method of lifting two-dimensional prints is to use an electrostatic dust lifter. This device works on many different surfaces whether they are porous or nonporous. The imprint residue must be extremely dry, never have been exposed to moisture, and must be on a clean surface. Any attempt to lift an impression that is wet or has ever been wet will result in a poor lift or none at all. Using an electrostatic lifting device on a dirty surface that contains other loose residue will result in the print and the "background" residue to be lifted simultaneously and thus the footwear impression will be lost. To conduct an electrostatic lift, a film is placed over the dusty print and attached at each corner to the surface with tape. The film has two distinct sides; one is black, and the other is metal. The black side of the film is placed against the surface of the print. A lead ground antenna is then positioned near the lifting film, but not so close that it may come into contact with the film. The power to the electrostatic lifter is then turned on and the tip of the red probe is touched to the silver side of the lifting film. While the probe is still touching the film, a roller may be used to gently apply maximum contact between the film and the surface. The device is then turned off. The probe should be held on the film for a few more seconds to allow it to discharge. The amount of time that is required for the charging of the impression varies according to the amount of residue. The lifting film should be handled very carefully and should be kept as flat as possible. The black side of the film should then be examined using oblique lighting and subsequently photographed (Bodziak 2000).

### *Collection of Impression Evidence*

Three-dimensional footwear impression evidence is collected by casting the print. There are several different types of materials that may be used to create the cast, but the casting procedures are very similar. Some of the materials are more durable than others, while some provide more detail of the impression.

One of the most common casting materials used is plaster of Paris. Plaster of Paris requires 90 oz. of water to 5 lbs. of plaster. Additional water may be added so that the mixture has a more fluid consistency. This type of casting material requires that a form or mold be placed around the impression so that it does not drain away from the print into a thin layer of plaster. Also, reinforcement material, such as metal wire, is necessary to prevent the cast from breaking upon lifting. When the shoe impression is located in loose dirt or sand, it should be pretreated with non-aerosol hair spray or dirt hardener spray before pouring the plaster to prevent any movement of particles during the casting process. The mixture should not be poured directly onto the print as it may obliterate the print. It should be poured near the impression and allowed to flow over the impression. After pouring half of the mixture, the reinforcement material should be put in place. The rest of the casting material should then be poured on top of the reinforcement material. The cast should dry for at least 45 to 60 minutes before it is lifted. For plaster of Paris, the cast should be allowed to dry at least 48 hours before cleaning (Hilderbrand 1999). Because plaster of Paris is prone to losing detail during cleaning, it should be cleaned very gently under running water. Figure 2.2 is an example of a plaster of Paris cast of a shoe impression in loose dirt.

Another type of casting material that is commonly used is dental stone. A few of the advantages of dental stone over plaster of Paris is that it provides more detail and is less prone to breakage. Also, it requires less time to harden and to set before cleaning. When preparing the dental stone mixture, 2 to 3 pounds of dental stone should be added to 12 to 15 ounces of water. Once again, the mixture should never be poured directly onto the impression. The dental stone cast should be allowed to dry at least 30 minutes before removal and allowed 24 hours to harden before cleaning (Hilderbrand 1999). Figure 2.3 is an example of a dental stone cast of a shoe impression in loose dirt.

If an impression is found in snow, it must be secured so that the impression is not obliterated during the casting process. One of the most common materials used is called Snow Print Wax©. This wax comes in an aerosol can so that it is easily applied to the

**Figure 2.2** Plaster of Paris Cast of Shoe Impression in Loose Dirt

**Figure 2.3** Dental Stone Cast of Shoe Impression in Loose Dirt

impression. It should be sprayed on the impression and allowed to dry before the pouring of the casting material. Also, Snow Print Wax© is colored so that it allows for greater contrast during photography. A form should then be placed around the print. The dental stone mixture should be prepared with very cold water and some snow from the area should be added to the mixture. This will prevent the snow in the impression from melting when the dental stone mixture is poured over it. The impression should then be covered and allowed to dry for 60 to 120 minutes before removal

(Hilderbrand 1999). The cast must then be allowed to dry for 48 hours.

When casting in water, a frame should be put around the impression that is high enough to not be completely submerged under water. Any material floating in the water that may interfere with or distort the cast should be removed. Dry dental stone should then be poured within the form until there is approximately a one inch layer covering the impression. A mixture of dental stone should then be made that is thicker than the mixture used on a normal footwear impression. This dental stone mixture should then be scooped into the frame and allowed 60 to 90 minutes to dry (Hilderbrand 1999). The cast should then be lifted and allowed to harden for 48 hours.

## Collection of Known Standards

To collect the sole patterns of known shoes, the bottom of the shoes should first be photographed with a scale. It is also important to recognize that there may be more sole wear on the standard shoes than there was at the time the scene impression was made. There are two methods of collecting standard shoe impressions. The first utilizes fingerprinting ink, and the second uses fingerprint powder.

To create a standard using fingerprinting ink, the ink should be rolled onto the bottom of the shoe using an ink roller. The sole can then either be rolled onto paper or the shoe can be stepped in and walked over paper. The amount of ink used on the bottom of the shoe should be minimal so as not to eliminate any individual characteristics through over-inking. Also, the inked shoe should be pressed onto paper multiple times to show all of the individual and class characteristics that may have been covered by ink on the first few tries.

To create a standard using fingerprint powder, the bottom of the standard shoe should be lightly dusted and pressed onto a clean sheet of adhesive tape or contact paper. Once the standard prints are made from known shoes, a comparison between the footwear evidence found at the scene and the standards can be examined. This can be done either by using a database or by visual examination.

## Conclusion

Footwear impressions are a valuable source of identification at a crime scene. Often this form of evidence is overlooked for several reasons. First, investigators are inadequately trained in the proper way to search and collect evidence. Second, the impressions could have been destroyed as a result of not securing the crime scene on first arrival to limit shoe impressions left by officers. Third, footwear impressions are undervalued in courts because there is a lack of knowledge about it. Also, latent impressions are often not collected or identified because they are simply not visible to the investigators, or they have been destroyed by bad weather conditions (Hilderbrand 1999).

When shoe impressions are identified as being present at a crime scene, a decision needs to be made of whether or not a print should be developed at the crime scene or taken back to the laboratory. Depending on the circumstances of the impression, it is preferable to take the impressions back to the lab; however, there are cases where this is not convenient. For example, when impressions have been left on pieces of shard glass or paper, the evidence should be transported carefully back to the laboratory to be examined thoroughly (Bodziak 2000, p. 99).

Factors to consider when deciding to perform a lifting or enhancing method on a two-dimensional impression is the type of surface features; porous, nonporous, dry, wet, clean, and dirty. The surface the impression is on such as plastic, paper, and/or fabric and the composition of the impression, wet residue, wet mud, grease, and blood are other issues to decide before a lift. The contrast of the surface and the impression, the presence of any materials such as dirt or grease which can interfere with the lifting process are factors that need to be considered. Moisture and humidity also affect the outcome of a lift (Bodziak 2000, p. 100).

When considering what type of casting materials should be used for three-dimensional impressions, the investigator should choose casting materials that reproduce fine detail, flows evenly into the impression, and can be cleaned without loss of detail. Cost effectiveness, a reasonable set time, no excess of equipment, and no limited shelf life are some other issues to consider when deciding on a casting material (Bodziak 2000, p. 67). Dental stone and Hard Core Blue have been proven to be good casting materials for three-dimensional footwear impressions because they meet these requirements.

Once footwear impressions have been cast and lifted, a comparison is made between a standard shoe and the suspect's shoe impression. There are several different databases that store standard shoe patterns, which can narrow the field of possible shoes that committed the crime. The different types of databases range from storing images of shoe designs from different manufacturers to storing images from crime scenes for the purpose of linking crimes (Bodziak 2000, pp. 284–285). An image-related database classification system was developed for shoe sole pattern designs. This classification code system includes preliminary and feature classification. The preliminary system is for shoe sole pattern designs and full shoe sole impressions. The feature classification is designed for partial footwear impressions and the codes for both classes are based on basic shapes (Astikainen and Mikkonen 1994).

The comparison process involves the seizing and examining of a suspect's shoes. If the crime was committed several months prior to the seizing of the shoes, then documentation and photographs of the shoes will need to be taken. The original impression itself is the best evidence, but it might need to be treated to enhance details. If the original impression is not available, then the original photographs taken at the crime scene are enlarged to natural size so that a comparison can be made (Bodziak 2000). It is viable that good casts, lifts, and photographs be taken on two- and three-dimensional footwear impressions so that in court the testimony and evidence presented will illustrate to the judge and jury that the footwear impression was either created or not created by the culprit.

## References

ASTIKAINEN, T., and S. MIKKONEN. 1994. Database classification system for shoe sole patterns—identification of partial footwear impression found at a scene of crime. *Journal of Forensic Sciences, 39,* 1227–1236.

BODZIAK, W. J. 2000. *Footwear impression evidence: Detection, recovery, and examination* (2nd ed.). Boca Raton, FL: CRC Press.

BODZIAK, W. J. 2005. Forensic footwear evidence. In S. James and J. Nordby (Eds.), *Forensic science: An introduction to scientific and investigative techniques* (2nd ed., pp. 361–375). Boca Raton, FL: CRC Press.

FISHER, B., A. SVENSSON, and O. WENDEL. 1981. *Techniques of crime scene investigation* (3rd ed.). NY: Elsevier North Holland, Inc.

HILDERBRAND, D. S. 1999. *Footwear, the missed evidence: A field guide to the collection and preservation of forensic footwear impression evidence.* Wildomar, CA: Staggs Publishing.

# 3

# Tire Impressions

*Ryan D. Mudd and James Warkentine*

## Introduction

Locard's exchange principle named after a French police officer, states that whenever two objects come into contact, trace materials are exchanged between the two. This principle can be applied to any object at a crime scene such as biological evidence, trace amounts of fibers, and prints, including but not limited to fingerprints, tire impressions, and tire tracks (Fisher 1981). Tire impressions have been used in many cases to both implicate and, more importantly, exonerate suspects related to a crime scene.

Today's society relies heavily upon automobiles as a main source of transportation. It can be generalized from this observation that wherever a crime is committed, an automobile most likely has some sort of involvement related to the crime or the criminal himself. In the majority of cases, the suspect either drove to or from the crime scene. If this is true, Locard's exchange principle should then be applicable to these tire impressions. Tire impressions and tracks are more often than not left at a crime scene as vehicles drive over dirt roads, snow, mud, or any other type of pliable surface. These impressions and prints are crucial in proving that a suspect's vehicle was at a crime scene (Bodziak 2005).

Tire treads are composed of many different components which give a tire a unique design. The designs left in tire impressions show many class and individual characteristics. Design elements are arranged in patterns or rows around the circumference of the tire and are commonly separated from one another by raised areas called grooves. Like design elements, grooves can also contain unique designs. Another component of the tire that distinguishes design elements are "sipes." Sipes are very small raised areas located in the design elements (Bodziak 2005). The design of these components is important when studying a suspect's tire impression. They convey important class characteristics which can enable investigators to determine the type of tire that possibly created this impression.

There is an immense discrepancy between tire impressions and tire tracks. Although both are mutually beneficial, they involve

49

different techniques in identifying a suspect's vehicle. Tire impressions give an accurate three-dimensional representation of a tire. They demonstrate the wear, dimensions, and design of a tire. A high quality tire impression acts as a footprint in that it depicts an array of class characteristics and, more importantly, individual characteristics (McDonald 1989, pp. 10–11). Class characteristics display that a particular print is a certain model created by a particular manufacturer, whereas individual characteristics can be used to show an exact match.

In an impression containing diminutive detail, these class characteristics can aid an investigation by revealing the type of tire found on a suspect's vehicle. For example, two tire prints produced by different brand new Michelin tires of identical size, type, and make will have numerous similar class characteristics. Individual characteristics are revealed in much more detailed prints and can be used to directly link a tire print to a particular tire involved with a crime scene (Bodziak 2005). These can be expressed if the impression contains signs of unique weathering, markings, or blemishes. By examining individual characteristics, two tires of the same model and manufacturer can be distinguished from one another.

Tire tracks are equally imperative in identifying a vehicle. A standard tire track is composed of, but not limited to, at least one set of tracks from the same vehicle. They can show many features of an unknown vehicle that a single tire impression cannot. Whereas a tire impression provides critical information regarding a vehicle's tire, the tire tracks present facts concerning the vehicle itself by offering the dimensions between the suspect's tracks. In studying and analyzing the tracks, it may be possible for a skilled technician to determine the vehicle's turning radius, track width, size, type, and wheelbase. This information can point investigators in the right direction in regard to matching the tracks and impressions to a particular vehicle (Bodziak 2005).

Many different types of databases exist that may further help officers identify a particular brand of tire. For instance, Pearl Communications has released a version of both *Tread Design Guide* by Tire Guides, Inc. and *Who Makes It and Where* on a CD-ROM. This CD contains photographs of more than 18,000 tire designs and information regarding their manufacturers. Another tool commonly used by investigators is a database created by the Michigan State Police and the Royal Canadian Mounted Police. This database collects vehicular information concerning tire tracks and can be used to obtain a list of probable vehicles (Bodziak 2005, p. 382).

Although prints and impressions are both mentioned when pertaining to the identification of a tire, they are entirely different. Tire prints, also referred to as residue prints, are two-dimensional markings usually found on pieces of paper, curbs, or cement (which are composed of dust particles). They can also be composed of water and various other mediums as a tire is passed through them and consequently abandons the residual medium in the form of a print (Given, Nehrich & Shields 1977, pp. 18–19). Residue prints can be lifted with adhesive paper in much the same way as fingerprints.

Tire impressions are dissimilar in that they are three-dimensional and are usually located in soil where they are collected in the form of a plaster cast. However, the location of these prints is not solely bound to soil; they are also found in snow and other malleable surfaces. Upon entering a crime scene and its surrounding areas, an investigator must keep a watchful eye for any and all impressions. In lieu of an impression's extremely fragile nature, it should be immediately recognized, photographed under various lighting, and properly lifted by trained technicians as to preclude the contamination of the impression.

During the lifting process, it is important that the tire impressions being lifted were actually produced by the suspect's vehicle. During a crime scene investigation many vehicles travel to and from the scene leaving useless and confusing tire impressions. Although precautionary measures should be reinforced to prevent this contamination, these prints are usually inevitable. Therefore, it is necessary for the investigators to distinguish between the known and unknown tire impressions (Bodziak 2005).

As an investigator examining tire impressions, it is important to create sketches of these impressions to show their relation to each other. It is nearly impossible to obtain too much information from a crime scene. Sketches, photographs, videos, and casts should all be produced to capture the originality of the crime scene. At this stage nothing should be overlooked and all impressions should be treated as valuable pieces of information (McDonald 1989). This can prove to be a tedious and extensive job depending on the number of impressions left at a crime scene.

Different surfaces require different lifting techniques. For instance, a tire impression found in snow would not be lifted in the same manner as an impression found on a muddy road. Depending on the nature of the impression and the media holding the impression, different techniques are frequently used in varying crime scenes. Because there is overwhelming variability involved in collecting and analyzing the impression, there is a need for a highly trained technician to choose the technique required to make an accurate lift.

In the past century, the value of tire tracks as evidence has risen drastically. Vehicles play an important role in 75% of all major crimes in today's society (Given, Nehrich & Shields 1977). In many cases, there is little apparent evidence at a crime scene other than fingerprints, a few footprints, and, more often than not, tire prints.

It is extremely important that tire impression experts understand the function of the tire, its components, and have full knowledge concerning the various methods of lifting an impression. Some of this information can be taught or studied, but a vast amount can only come through years of dedication and hands-on experience.

Tire impressions are most commonly used for identification purposes. By using tire impressions for comparison purposes, a suspect and his or her vehicle may be linked to a crime scene. Tire marks and impressions can do so much more than that, though;

they can provide valuable information about an unknown vehicle such as: the direction it traveled, the type of vehicle that was driven, and what/where the car may have traveled over. On damp surfaces the layer of ground on which the wheel rolls is compacted. As the wheel rolls forward the compacted dirt is lifted in the direction the wheel is going (Fisher 1981). This is useful for determining the direction a vehicle is traveling.

If a vehicle passes two divergent surfaces, direction can be determined from the transference of materials from the first surface onto the second. This relates directly to Locard's exchange principle. For example, a truck is traveling on a damp dirt road. A short distance later, the dirt road abruptly ends and connects directly onto an asphalt road. The tires will have left marks from the dirt road directly onto the asphalt. As the truck continues to travel, the marks will diminish. Direction of travel can be determined if a vehicle travels through a puddle of water. Assuming that the vehicle was traveling at a reasonable speed, the water from the puddle should dissipate and splash onto the surrounding surface in the direction the vehicle was traveling (Given, Nehrich & Shields 1977).

Skid marks are important types of tire marks and are commonly relied upon in hit-and-runs, homicides, and robberies. By analyzing a skid mark an expert can determine a vehicle's minimum speed and the direction of travel (Given, Nehrich & Shields 1977). Although these details do not provide investigators with information regarding a suspect's car, they may prove useful in recreating the events of the crime.

A trained technician can accurately determine the type of car that left a tire impression by examining certain aspects of the impression such as its circumference, tread width, and turning diameter. To determine the circumference of a tire, find an individual characteristic in the print and measure the distance between that specific point and the point at which that individual characteristic appears again. This measurement is equal to the rolling tire circumference. In conjunction with the tire circumference, it is important to obtain the tread width. This is the measurement in width for the tire impression. Knowing both the tire circumference and tread width, tire manufacturers are able to determine the size of the tire (McDonald 1989).

The turning diameter of a vehicle can also be determined from tire tracks. If a substantial track is left at a crime scene which shows a tight turning arc, a measurement can be made of this to help determine the turning diameter. The chord (the tight arc measured from the outside front tire) is first measured followed by the center of the chord at the point of which it is closest to the arc. This is illustrated in Figure 3.1. The investigator can then submit these measurements to a laboratory such as the East Lansing Forensic Laboratory where the turning diameter will be determined or it can be calculated by using the following formula: Turning diameter = $2(C^2/8M + M/2)$. However, most authorities agree that this

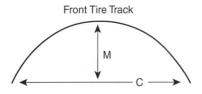

Front Tire Track

M

C

The chord (C) is measured followed by
the distance from the center of chord to
the closest point on the art.

**Figure 3.1**   Measurement of Turning Diameter

technique should not be used to identify vehicles, only to eliminate suspect vehicles (McDonald 1989, p. 70).

"The ultimate goal of tire track investigation is the identification of the vehicle producing the track. If sufficient tire track information is present, careful and accurate measurements can yield both the manufacturer and the production year of the suspect vehicle" (Given, Nehrich & Shields 1977, p. 6). The use of tire impressions to identify suspect vehicles has increased through the past few decades. In today's automotive world most crimes deal with the need for tire impression analysis. Trained technicians should thoroughly understand and implement the techniques and procedures for accurately processing tire impression evidence. Through the understanding of the mentioned techniques and hands-on training, investigators and technicians have helped implicate criminals and exonerate the innocent.

## Collection and Preservation of Tire Impressions

### *Documentation of Tire Impression Evidence*

When left at a crime scene, all tire impression evidence should be thoroughly recorded and documented. The manner of collection and preservation of an impression is dependent on the medium upon which the impression is made. The sequential steps that should be taken in any situation requiring documentation should be first to photograph the print in its original form, then stabilize the print and rephotograph, and finally cast or lift the impression (Bodziak 2000).

### *Photography*

Before any collection procedures are performed on the impression, the imprint staging area should be photographically recorded with a 35mm camera. The first series of photographs should be taken at a distance to orient the position of the impression geographically in the scene as shown in Figure 3.2. After these photographs are taken, the next series should be taken at an intermediate range to document the impression in its immediate surroundings. Finally, the last series of photographs should be close-range to document

**Figure 3.2**  Distant Photo of Tire Tracks in Dirt Roadway

the actual characteristics of the tire impression as shown in Figure 3.3 (Bodziak 2000).

When photographing the close-range details of the impression, certain measures should be taken to ensure proper documentation. The two most important rules to remember when taking close-range photographs is orienting the camera properly in relation to the impression, and omitting the use of camera-mounted flash (Bodziak 2000). When the photo is taken, the camera should be situated on a tripod with the camera's focal line perpendicular to the surface upon or into which the impression was made. In different lighting situations, it may be necessary to block out natural light and situate oblique lighting or flash 2 to 3 feet on the periphery of the impression in order to enhance ridge details. To arrange oblique lighting, one should position the light sources in such a way that the corresponding angle between the two is approximately 180 degrees. In relation to the ground, the two light sources should be 10 to 40 degrees as shown in Figures 3.4 and 3.5 (Bodziak 2000).

A scale model that is labeled with a case number should then be placed adjacent to the impression and at the same level as the base of the print. To document the class characteristics of the tire impression, the photograph should focus primarily on the impression itself with the scale model clearly visible.

**Figure 3.3**  Intermediate Photo of Tire Impression in Dirt Roadway

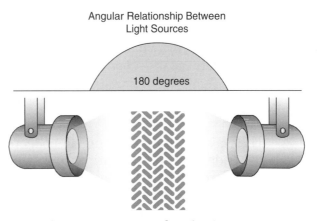

**Figure 3.4**  Angular Positioning of Light Source

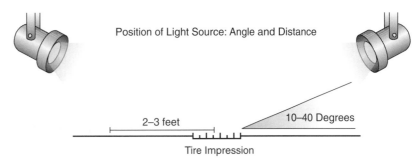

**Figure 3.5**  Position of Light Source in Relation to Tire Impression

### *Scene Sketching*

Before working to lift the impression, it is important to make a sketch of the scene. The purpose of this is to document clearly the location of evidence relative to major points within the scene. In addition to serving as an aid to refresh the memory of the investigator, it also visually documents the layout of the scene for the casual observer.

When preparing a sketch, the artist first needs to choose permanent fixtures within the scene and clearly position them in the sketch. These fixtures will serve as stationary reference points to triangulate the positions of impressions and all other evidentiary elements (Miller 2005). With the reference points and all evidentiary elements shown and the measurements between the two clearly defined, one is able to accurately depict the layout of the scene. It should be noted that it is not necessary for the scene to be drawn to scale. As long as the parts of the scene are in the correct position relative to one another and portray an accurate depiction of the scene itself, the drawing will suffice (Miller 2005).

Within the margin of the rough sketch, information should be included that provides details of the scene and the background of the sketch. This information specifies the case number, nature of the scene, address of the scene, artist's name, and the date and time the scene was sketched (Miller 2005). If there are additional elements in the scene that require more detail to define, they are usually numbered on the sketch and listed in a legend. Within the legend, specific details about the numbered elements are given. By positioning this extraneous information on the margins of the sketch, rather than on the drawn sketch itself, less visual disturbance is produced and a concise representation of the scene remains (Miller 2005).

## Methods of Collection

The way in which evidence is collected at the crime scene is highly dependent on the medium upon which the impression was made. When an impression is made in a medium that will yield to the weight of the automobile, a three-dimensional impression will result. By definition, this impression will have a length, width, and depth vector. However, if the imprinting medium is nonyielding, a two-dimensional impression will be created. The impression left in this instance will have the same length and width vector, but the depth vector will be nonexistent. It is important to understand the difference between these two types of impressions, because the collection methods used for each type are dissimilar.

In most three-dimensional impressions, dental stone, or a similar casting material, can be used to cast the impression with good results, but there may be changes in the overall technique depending on the consistency of the imprinting material. Impressions that are made in media that have higher water content require an extended drying time for proper casting (Hilderbrand 1999). Impressions left in snow can be cast in the same general manner as other three-dimensional prints. However, the snow impression must first be treated with Snow Print Wax© and then cast with dental stone or melted sulfur (Warrington 2005). Impressions made in dry material require the application of a congealing compound, such as hair spray or dirt hardener, to set the loose material and prevent the destruction of the impression while the casting material is being poured (Hilderbrand 1999).

Two-dimensional prints are usually laid down as residual prints. This type of print results when a tire passes through one type of media and then deposits the material onto another surface. Prints of this nature can be lifted and preserved with the use of adhesive or gelatin lifters if the impression is laid in a medium that is of a dry nature. For impressions that are of a wet nature, only gelatin lifters can be employed to lift the print (Bodziak 2000).

### Collection of Residual Imprint Evidence

For the most part, gelatin lifters and adhesive tape use the same technique to lift a residual print (Bodziak 2000). To perform the technique, a light dusting with fingerprint powder can be applied to the impression for enhancement. The adhesive lifter is then applied to the impression, adhesive side down, and then gently rolled to pick up the small particles in the impression (Bodziak 2000). The print is then peeled back to lift the impression. After the impression is lifted, a reverse image is left on the adhesive side of the tape. This image should be quickly photographed to record the impression and then covered with an acetate sheet to protect the impression for further examination. In some cases, crystal violet or other dyes can be applied to the adhesive tape for improved enhancement; however, this technique of dyeing the impression may not be used with the gelatin lifters (Bodziak 2000).

When an impression is made in a material that is of a wet origin, only a gelatin lifter may be used. The process needed for use of this lifting device is the same as the technique described in the previous paragraph. It is important to note that a gelatin lifter can be used on a wider array of surfaces and with a larger spectrum of impression materials; therefore, it is a very useful tool for lifting residue impressions.

## Collection of Three-Dimensional Impression Evidence

### Technique for Casting Three-Dimensional Impressions

Three-dimensional impressions result when the surface upon which the impression is made yields to the weight of the automobile. In this case, the impression should be recorded with casting materials such as dental stone or plaster of Paris (Hilderbrand 1999). To cast an impression with plaster of Paris, a ratio of 90 ounces of water to 5 pounds of casting materials is needed to make a mixture that is viscous enough to suffuse the impression and record the impression's fine details (Hilderbrand 1999). Before pouring the plaster of Paris into the impression, the dirt particles should be stabilized with the dirt hardener or hairspray (Bodziak 2000). This precautionary measure is used to prevent the destruction of the impression when the casting material is spread upon the loose particles of the impression. See Figures 3.6 and 3.7.

After the impression is hardened, a mold should be constructed to retain the liquid casting material. With the mold in place, the plaster should be poured in such a way that it is able to enter the impression from the periphery without disturbing the particles of the impression (Hilderbrand 1999). After allowing the casting material to remain undisturbed in the impression for approximately 1 hour, the plaster should be removed from the impression and stored in open air for at least 2 days before any initial cleaning is performed (Hilderbrand 1999). To clean the impression, only water should be allowed to gently flow over the surface of the cast to remove any dirt particles that remain. It should be noted that for no reason shall abrasive cleaning methods be used on this type of cast. Such rough treatment would obliterate the fine details collected by the casting. See Figure 3.8.

Care should be taken when handling a cast made from plaster of Paris, because it has low compression strength. This makes the cast more fragile than casts made with other casting materials (Bodziak 2000). To prevent breakage, it should be stored in a porous container and handled only by laboratory examiners.

**Figure 3.6** Brick Mold Surrounding a Portion of a Tire Impression

**Figure 3.7** Plaster in Brick Mold

**Figure 3.8** Tire Impression Cast

The procedure to cast with dental stone is similar to that of the plaster of Paris with a few notable exceptions. First, the ratio of the dental stone is approximately 3 pounds of casting material to 12 to 15 ounces of water (Hilderbrand 1999). Also, there is no need to build a mold to retain the casting mixture. However, personal experiments have shown that having a mold may lend itself to achieving better results. Because the compression strength of dental stone is nearly eight times that of plaster of Paris, 8000 psi to 1200 psi, respectively, the durability of dental stone is much higher (Bodziak 2000). Also, there is less time required for the cast to set. After one day, the dental stone will reach its optimum compression strength and be ready for cleaning.

In addition to quicker setting time, the dental stone also allows for more enhanced detail analysis than plaster of Paris. Consequently, the dental stone is the superior casting material for casting tire impression evidence because of its reliability, durability, and efficiency of use. In terms of cost, however, plaster of Paris might be the wiser choice. A 25-pound package of plaster of Paris has been found to be two to four times less expensive than dental stone in the same quantity (Special Affect Supply Corporation 2005).

### Technique for Casting Impression in Snow

The procedure for casting impressions in snow is similar to casting regular three-dimensional impressions in dry material; however, extra steps are needed to prevent the destruction of the impression during the casting process. Before the casting material is poured onto the impression, the impression must be set with an aerosol wax spray, commonly referred to as Snow Print Wax©, to prevent the casting material from damaging the impression (Hilderbrand 1999).

The Snow Print Wax© must be applied to the print with three applications that are separated by one-minute intervals and then left undisturbed for ten minutes. After the wax has set, dental stone should be mixed in the ratio described previously. Because using regular water to mix the dental stone would be create a mixture that would have a temperature too high to apply to snow, it would be wiser to use the snow from the surrounding area as the water source for the dental stone mixture (Warrington 2005). By doing so, the temperature of the mixture would be sufficiently lowered, thereby decreasing the probability of the snow impression melting away during the application. After the dental stone mixture is applied to the impression, the casting material should be covered and allowed to harden for approximately two hours before removal. After the cast is removed from the scene, it should be allowed to dry for two days to reach its full hardness potential.

Another way to cast the print involves the use of melted sulfur in combination with Snow Print Wax© (Warrington 2005). With this process, the wax is applied in the same manner as with the dental stone. After allowing the wax to remain undisturbed for ten minutes, the sulfur is melted in a pot with constant stirring. After all of the sulfur has melted, it must be set aside and allowed to cool until it almost reaches its crystallization point. Before the sulfur has a chance to crystallize, quickly pour the mixture directly onto the waxed impression. The temperature of the snow will quickly harden the cast.

Although the bottom portion of the cast crystallizes quickly, it is best to wait approximately 30 minutes before handling or removing the cast. This will allow the entire cast to cure and also help maintain the integrity of the cast. Due to the brittle nature of the sulfur cast, extreme care should be taken when handling at this point (Warrington 2005).

### Technique for Casting Impressions in Moist Sand or Dirt

With the presence of extra moisture in the imprinting material, extra steps must be taken to allow the casting material to dry and completely cure. One simple solution to this problem is to allow the casting material approximately one extra hour within the impression before its removal (Hilderbrand 1999). Another solution would be to decrease the amount of water used in the casting mixture (Bodziak 2000). With the extra moisture in the medium making the casting mixture more diluted, one can simply decrease, by one-half ounce, the amount of water added to the casting mixture prior to its application to the impression. The extra moisture in the medium would then be absorbed by the casting mixture to make the ratio between water and casting material more optimum.

## Collection of Known Standards

The main reason to collect tire impression evidence at the scene of a crime is to compare it to a known standard that belongs to a suspected perpetrator. If not for the chance to make this comparison, nothing done in the previous sections would be worth the time and effort involved. Therefore, the discovery and analysis of known standards are of supreme importance.

One very common way to produce a known standard is to apply a light application of fingerprint powder to the outside treads of the tire. After application, the tire is then rolled over a length of contact paper and a track image of the tire is produced. With a light application of the fingerprint powder applied to the tire, the individual characteristics of the tire will be clearly visible (Bodziak 2000).

Another method involves the use of fingerprint ink rather than powder. A light application is spread over the treads of the tire which is also rolled over contact paper. With this method, it is important not to apply too much ink to the treads of the tire. The over-application of ink would cause the fine details of the print to be lost (Bodziak 2000).

A new method of collecting known standards is accomplished with the use of carbon carrier sheets that are connected to an adhesive image receiving sheet of paper. This system, which transfers a carbon image from the carbon carrier sheet to the adhesive image receiving sheet, allows a standard to be made while the tires are still fixed to the automobile. The sheets are simply placed in the path of the tires, and the car is allowed to roll over them. The weight of the car then compresses the two sheets together, and the resulting image made by the details of the tire is transferred from the carbon sheet to the adhesive sheet (GSA 2005).

When the known standard is produced, the details of the tire are compared to those left by the suspect vehicle. If the impression lifted or cast at the crime scene matches the known standard impression produced in the laboratory, more suspicion may be placed upon the alleged perpetrator of the crime. More often than not, however, this process is used in the field of forensic science to exclude suspected criminals rather than playing an inculpatory role.

# References

BODZIAK, W. J. 2005. Forensic footwear evidence. In S. James and J. Nordby (Eds.), *Forensic science: An introduction to scientific and investigative techniques* (2nd ed., pp. 361–375). NY: Taylor and Francis.

BODZIAK, W. J. 2000. *Footwear impression evidence: Detection, recovery, and examination* (2nd ed). NY: CRC Press.

FISHER, B., A. SVENNSON, and O. WENDEL. 1981. *Techniques of crime scene investigation* (3rd ed.). NY: Elsevier North Holland, Inc.

GIVEN, B., R. NEHRICH, and J. SHIELDS. 1977. *Tire tracks and tread marks.* Houston, TX: Gulf Publishing Company.

GSA Law Enforcement Associates Corporation. 2005. *Locating and protecting impression evidence.* Retrieved November 18, 2005, from http://leacorp.com/pdfs/Forensic_Supply_Products/5_impression.pdf

HILDERBRAND, D. S. 1999. *Footwear, the missed evidence: A field guide to the collection and preservation of forensic footwear impression evidence.* Wildomar, CA: Staggs Publishing.

McDONALD, P. 1989. *Tire imprint evidence.* NY: Elsevier North Holland, Inc.

MILLER, M. T. 2005. *Crime scene investigation.* In S. James and J. Nordby (Eds), *Forensic science: An introduction to scientific and investigative techniques* (2nd ed., pp. 174–176). NY: CRC Press.

Special Affect Supply Corporation. 2005. *Plaster, stone, and gypsum products.* Retrieved November 10, 2005, from http://www.fxsupply.com/material/plaster.html

WARRINGTON, R. 2005. *Casting in snow with sulfur.* Retrieved November 18, 2005, from http://www.csigizmos.com/products/toolingimpressionmaterial/sulfur.html

# 4

# Bite Marks

*Stephanie Rollins and Wendi Sanders*

## Introduction

Dental impressions are primarily used for two reasons in relation to the field of forensic science. The first, which will not be discussed in this chapter, involves the use of an individual's dentition as a means to identify a person as well as a potential source for DNA. The second, and the focus of this chapter, involves the use of a bite mark to identify an assailant in a crime. These bite marks are most often the result of crimes such as rape, murder, child abuse, and spousal abuse (Bowers 2004).

There are many times in history where dental evidence has been used as a means of identification. Some sources reveal that certain nobility used their bite mark impression as their symbol on the sealing wax of a letter during the eleventh century. The first court case reported to hold bite mark evidence admissible was *Doyle v. State* in 1954. In this particular case, which occurred in Texas, a dentist compared bite marks left on two separate pieces of cheese to the known plaster model dentition of the defendant. Other landmark cases where bite mark evidence was deemed admissible include *People v. Marx (1975), Niehaus v. State of Indiana (1977),* and *State v. Sager* (1980) (Bowers 2004). In each of these unique cases, bite mark evidence was deemed a reliable science, thus placing it under Daubert standards, as established in *Daubert v. Merrell Dow Pharmaceuticals* (1995).

When evaluating bite marks, one must consider two different types of characteristics: class and individual. Class characteristics constitute a wide range of different features and in bite mark evidence generally characterize a different group of teeth, such as incisors or molars, and whether the teeth are located on the upper or lower jaws. Individual characteristics allow a bite mark to be linked to a specific individual and include damaged or broken teeth or a misalignment of the teeth. It is these characteristics that allow a bite mark to be identified as unique and a match to a specific individual (Stimson and Mertz 1997, pp. 137–158).

There are many different types of surfaces that a bite mark could be present upon that can be found at a crime scene. These include surfaces such as fruit, cheese, gum, and human skin or tissue (Furuhata and Yamamoto 1967). Each surface will produce bite marks of different qualities and clarity, depending on their hardness and consistency. It is imperative in a criminal investigation that any surface that could have received a dentition be examined thoroughly in order to acquire the bite mark.

Depending on how the bite occurred, each bite mark can result in unique patterns on the surface that received the bite. Generally, bite marks occurring on human skin cause hemorrhaging around the dentition, but the extent of the bruising can vary depending on the fragility level of an individual's capillaries located near the surface of the skin. This bruising can be a result of the actual pressure exerted on the skin by the teeth themselves or can be due to what is referred to as "negative pressure," a direct consequence of sucking by the assailant. Oftentimes, the bite mark can cause swelling of the skin and tissue. This can cause distortion of the bite mark so one must be careful when trying to acquire this type of evidence. In the most severe cases, skin may even be removed from the victim's body due to the great force exerted during the bite from the assailant. Another unique feature that could occur from a bite mark is termed *drag marks*.

Drag marks are a result of the movement of the teeth over the surface that receives the bite mark. Double patterns can be seen in some cases and are a consequence of the biter consecutively biting the same area in a very short amount of time so that the skin does not have adequate time to recede back to its normal position. Patterns can also result from a bite mark, especially if there is a median surface such as a piece of cloth present between the teeth and the surface upon which the bite mark is occurring (Stimson and Mertz 1997, pp. 137–158).

Another factor to consider when evaluating bite marks on human skin or tissue is the possible time of death. *Antemortem*, or before death, bite marks tend to cause a large amount of diffuse bruising, whereas *perimortem*, or within 5 minutes of death, bite marks tend to cause a well-defined bruising pattern that is not quite as diffuse as that of antimortem marks. Another type occurs *postmortem*, or after death. These particular dentitions have indentions but due to the fact that the heart is no longer pumping and, consequently, blood is not circulating, bruising does not result. Postmortem bite marks are thus harder to identify (Moenssens and Inbau 1978; Glass 2005, pp. 79–98). Bite marks can also be either defensive or offensive. Defensive bite marks tend to be less defined in nature and tearing of the skin often occurs whereas offensive bite marks have well-defined bite patterns, usually single in nature, contrasted to double patterns (Glass 2005, pp. 79–98).

Yet another important point to remember when investigating bite mark evidence is the time that has passed since the bite mark was made. Because human skin and tissue is very elastic, as time progresses the bite mark clarity tends to decrease and bruising due to the pressure exerted by the teeth tends to become more diffuse until it eventually dissipates. Therefore, photographs should be taken of the bite mark in a timely manner in order to ensure an accurate depiction of the bite mark.

The length of time that a bite mark will be present tends to vary from person to person and has many other variables such as the changing posture of the victim. Generally, bite marks that do not tear the skin can last anywhere from 3 minutes to 24 hours. Depending on the area that was the target of the bite mark and when the skin was penetrated by the pressure of the teeth, the marks can last from one to three days. Also, bite mark longevity varies due to the location the bite mark was made and even from women to men. Due to these inconsistencies, an exact time that the bite mark occurred might not be able to be made, but there is a window in which this bite mark evidence must be collected or else it will be lost (Moenssens and Inbau 1978).

It is very important to realize that when analyzing bite mark evidence there is a possibility that DNA may be present. Saliva is often deposited at a bite mark by the assailant so a swabbing should be made of the area before any further techniques are employed to acquire either a cast of or the actual bite mark itself. The DNA evidence is more valuable than the bite mark itself so one should make sure to execute the swabbing of the bite mark area (Forensic Dentistry Online 2005, para 3).

Following you will find many different techniques often employed to produce casts of bite marks left on victims and other objects, as well as dentitions of the suspects. As with any evidence collection, there are some important things to remember. First, quality photographs need to be taken. These will be vital in order to accurately perform overlays of the suspect's dentition and the bite mark located on the victim or other object. Also, as mentioned in the previous paragraph, DNA evidence is paramount and must be the priority in a bite mark case. Swabbings of the bite mark area should be taken and immediately sent to the laboratory for analysis. Finally, care must be taken when attempting to lift a cast of a bite mark or dentition. Sufficient time must elapse before lifting the cast, otherwise the cast will be null and another cast will be necessary.

## Bite Marks

Teeth, just like tools, can be used as weapons (Forensic Dentistry Online 2005 A). Therefore, there needs to be a basic standard methodology for forensic dentists to follow to ensure that the quality, validity, collection, preservation, and analysis of the evidence found in bite mark cases can be established (McNamee and Sweet 2003). Forensic odontology, or forensic dentistry, is an emerging field that is not just used for identifying victims, especially burn victims, by their dental records. It is also being used as a standard way to identify assailants by comparing their dentition to impressions of bite marks left on victims in cases that involve bite mark evidence. The forensic dentists can match the impression on a victim to the tooth structures from a suspect. The theory behind this field is not new. It relates back to the fact that no two individuals have the exact same dentition and that teeth, due to their individual characteristics, leave recognizable marks (Dorion 2005). It is known that this field is always changing and expanding with new techniques. However, this chapter will discuss the standard protocol being used at the time of the publication of this manual set by the American Board of Forensic Odontology (ABFO) for collecting evidence in bite mark cases that "will aid in the unity and reliability of the profession" for many years to come (McNamee and Sweet 2003, p. 382).

### Description of the Bite Mark

When the odontologist examines the bite mark, the following information should be recorded (this is an excerpt from an ABFO Guidelines checklist in the Bitemark Evidence Text, pages 601–605):

A. **Demographics**
   a) Name of victim
   b) Case number
   c) Date of examination
   d) Person to contact
   e) Age of victim
   f) Race of victim
   g) Sex of victim
   h) Name of examiner

B. **Location of Bite Mark**
   a) Describe anatomical location
   b) Describe surface contour: flat, curved, irregular
   c) Describe tissue characteristics
      1. How deep is the bite? Into bone, cartilage, muscle, fat

C. **Shape**
   a) Round, ovoid, crescent, elliptical, irregular

D. **Color**
   a) Red, purple, and so on

E. **Size**
   a) Vertical and horizontal dimensions of the bite mark should be noted.

F. **Type of Injury:** there are seven types of bite marks listed and defined as:
   1. Hemorrhage—small bleeding spot
   2. Contusion—ruptured blood vessel, bruise
   3. Abrasion—undamaged mark on skin
   4. Laceration—punctured or torn skin
   5. Incision—neat puncture of skin
   6. Avulsion—removal of skin
   7. Artifact—bitten-off piece of body (Dorion 2005, pp. 601–605).

### *Evidence Collection from the Victim*

A. **Photography**
   1. Take numerous orientation and close-up photographs of the bite mark.
   2. A reference scale, ruler, should be placed in the photographs.
   3. Be sure in close-up photographs that the camera is positioned directly over the injury site.
   4. Specific lighting should be considered when taking these photographs. One may utilize off-angle lighting, oblique lighting and/or ultraviolet lighting to enhance the detail that will show up in the photographs.
   5. When taking photographs of evidence it is always good to have more photographs than not enough. That way all possible aspects of the evidence will be captured for record (Forensic Dentistry Online 2005 B).

B. **Saliva Swabs**
   When a forensic dentist is called to a scene or first encounters the victim, it needs to be determined if the bite mark has been cleaned or tampered with in any way. Because the forensic dentist is not usually the first to examine or see the evidence, sometimes alterations can occur before one can collect the evidence samples that are needed. During the actual bite, saliva will have been deposited on the victim's skin from the assailant. This should be collected for DNA analysis. If the bite site has not been washed, a saliva swab needs to be obtained. This is done by completing the following steps for the double swab technique:
   1. Get a cotton swab and moisten it with distilled water.
   2. Wash over the surface that was contacted by the tongue and lips during the bite with light pressure and circular motions.
   3. Use a second cotton swab that is dry to collect the moisture that is left on the skin by the first swab.
   4. Both swabs should be allowed to air dry at room temperature for at least 45 minutes before they are sent away for testing.
   5. Store the swabs in separate paper evidence envelopes or boxes that will allow air to continue to circulate around the swab tips. They should be kept cool and dry to prevent the degradation of the salivary DNA and to prevent the growth of bacteria that may contaminate the samples.
   *Note*: **The swabs should never be sealed in plastic bags or containers.**
   6. The swabs should be refrigerated or frozen during storage (Forensic Dentistry Online 2005 A).

C. **DNA Sample**
   A sample of DNA needs to be taken from the victim to provide the analyst the opportunity to compare the victim's DNA with

the sample from the bite mark. By doing so, if there is any mixture of DNA from the bite site swab, the victim's DNA can be differentiated from any suspect's DNA.
1. A buccal, or cheek, swab may be used.
    a) Use a sterile cotton swab to scrub the inside of the cheek.
    b) Preserve and store these swabs in the same manner as the saliva swabs.
    c) Make sure that there has been no food or drink for at least 20 minutes before the collection.
2. A sample of the victim's blood may also be taken (Dorion 2005).

The following impressions and casts need to be taken of the victim's teeth in order to rule out their dentition as the one that caused the bite marks. These pieces of evidence can also be used to compare with any defensive bite wounds that are found on any suspects.

**D. Impressions**
1. Victim's Sample Bite Impression—by using a wax substance or wafer the victim can bite down and leave their bite pattern for comparison purposes (Dorion 2005).
2. Victim's Dental Impression—An impression needs to be made of the victim's teeth by completing the following steps:
    a) Get the correct size impression trays, one upper and one lower, depending on the mouth size of the suspect in question.
    b) Measure out the correct amount of dental alginate and put it into a plastic bowl.
    c) Pour in the appropriate amount of water into the bowl. (Follow the directions for the proper ratio of alginate and water for the dental alginate that you are using).
    d) Mix the contents until there is a smooth mixture with no clumps or air bubbles.
    e) Fill the upper and lower impression trays with the alginate mixture. Work quickly so that the alginate does not begin to set.
    f) Once the trays are filled place one in the victim's mouth, and tell them to bite down hard for two minutes.
    g) Remove the tray and set it aside to finish setting.
    h) Now insert the second tray and repeat procedure.
    i) Once the alginate has set, one can move on to making the casts. Remember to leave the impressions in the trays when making the casts. These trays serve as backing for the materials (Dorion 2005).

**E. Casts**
1. Once the impressions have been made of the victim's teeth, casts need to be made following these steps:
    a) Dental stone is used to make casts from the alginate impressions. Follow the instructions that come with the

dental stone for the appropriate ratio of dental stone to water. First pour the dental stone powder into a plastic bowl.
b) Add water to the bowl.
c) Mix thoroughly to get all of the clumps out of the mixture.
d) Fill each of the alginate impressions with dental stone mixture. Be sure to press the mixture firmly to be sure to get into all of the spaces and "nooks and crannies" created by the teeth.
e) After the dental stone is in, tap the impressions to be sure that there are no air bubbles in the mixture.
f) Let the cast set for about 45 minutes.
g) After the dental stone has set, remove the cast and alginate impression from the trays. One can now peel away the alginate impression and throw it away. What is left is a cast model of the victim's teeth that can be used for comparison purposes to the bite marks that were created (Dorion 2005).

**F. Mold of the Bite Site**
1. Various dental materials are available that are of low viscosity and low consistency that can be used to make impressions of the bite marks that are left on a victim. Some examples are: vinyl polysiloxanes (VPS), Water Mark, Correct, Supersil, Aquasil, and Reprosil.
2. The instructions should be read for each different dental material used but the basic instructions are the same:
a) Mix the dental stone material being used with the appropriate ratio of powder to water. Be sure to get all of the bubbles and clumps out of the mix.
b) A ring needs to be made that can be placed around the bite site to hold the mold into place. TAK Hydroplastic is commonly used as the backing for bite mark impressions. It is a plastic that softens in hot water and it can be molded into a ring and rehardens in about 5–10 minutes.
c) Once the ring is in place, pour the mold over the bite mark and allow it to dry for the appropriate amount of time for the material that was used.
d) Remove the mold impression when it is completely dry.
e) The impression molds should be stored in a marked container, that is labeled with the case number, date, and so on (Dorion 2005, p. 6).

**G. Tissue Excision/Preservation**
1. In certain cases with deceased victims it may be necessary for a pathologist to use a more invasive technique of excising and preserving the bite mark itself. This would be done in order to preserve the bite mark in its original three-dimensional form which will allow the forensic dentist the opportunity to:
a) "do additional or future and direct analysis of the bite mark"

   b) perform additional "analysis of the relationship among the skin abrasions, erosions, perforations, etc., and the underlying tissue, the inflammatory response, subcutaneous hemorrhage"

   c) complete "direct comparison of the suspect dentition (dental casts) to the bite mark" (Dorion 2005, p. 225). This is extremely useful when a suspect is detained some time after the bite mark was created.

2. It is important to note that the decision to excise a bite mark is determined by the forensic dentist but is approved by the coroner/medical examiner/pathologist in the area that the case exists. One must be sure to go through the proper legal avenues in order to get permission to excise a bite mark that might lead to a conviction of a perpetrator.

3. Once the tissue is excised it will shrink by as much as 50% if it is not fixed to a ring for support and backing. Today TAK Hydroplastic is used for this ring fabrication. Once the bite mark is removed it can be attached to the backing with glue. This will keep the bite mark from distorting over time (Dorion 2005).

4. Once the tissue has been excised and supported with a ring it needs to be fixed or preserved in a formalin solution. Formalin is a solution that is 40% formaldehyde and 60% water. Today most tissues are fixed in a 10% formalin solution which is one part formalin and nine parts water. By fixing these tissues they will be well preserved for years to come (Dorion 2005).

5. After all of these steps have been completed the excised bite mark needs to be properly stored. The fixed supported excised bite mark needs to be stored in an identified plastic container with a lid or a sealed plastic bag. Preferably this evidence needs to be placed in a refrigerated unit. If it cannot be placed in a refrigerated unit then keeping it at room temperature is the next best thing.

6. As with all pieces of evidence, this process needs to be documented by taking multiple photographs throughout the entire process of excision, ring backing, fixation, and storage (Dorion 2005).

## Evidence Collection from the Suspect

Before any evidence is collected from any suspects the forensic dentist needs to be sure that the necessary warrants, court orders, or legal consent has been obtained so that any evidence collected will be admissible if the case goes to court.

### History/Dental Records

The dental records of a suspect should be obtained for comparison purposes. A history should be taken of any dental work performed subsequent to or around the date of the bite mark (Forensic Dentistry Online 2005 B). The United States has a well developed system of recording dental records. It is called the Universal System. In this system each tooth is numbered from one to thirty-two and the five surfaces of each tooth are classified. The dental records also contain information noting if the person has any fillings, extractions, root configuration, and/or twisted/tilted teeth. This will be useful if the forensic dentist needs to compare a suspect's records to a bite mark site (Forensic Dentistry Online 2005 A).

### Photography

1. Extraoral photographs
    a. Full face photographs
    b. Profile photographs
2. Intraoral photographs
    a. Frontal view
    b. Two lateral views (right and left)
    c. Views of each arch (upper and lower)

### Extraoral examination

1. Evidence of trauma, surgery and/or facial asymmetry should be documented.
2. In order to see the factors that influence biting dynamics, the joint status, muscle tone, and balance should all be noted.
3. Measure the maximum opening of the mouth.

### Intraoral examination

1. Missing or misaligned teeth should be noted.
2. Broken or restored teeth should be noted.
3. Previous dental records should be reviewed for comparison.
4. Tongue size and function should be noted.
5. A saliva swab should be taken from the suspect for DNA comparison if saliva evidence was taken from the bite on the victim (Forensic Dentistry Online 2005 B; Dorion 2005, pp. 607–609).

**Sample Bites** are used to visualize the pattern produced by the biting edges of the suspect's teeth to be compared to the bite mark itself.

1. Wax—test bites can be made in wax. Aluwax is currently the most common wax used. It comes in wafer form that suspects can bite down on to leave their bite impressions.
2. If a bite mark was left in an inanimate object at the crime scene, a cast could be made from this bite to use for future comparisons. For example, in numerous cases, bite marks have been left in different food stuffs (cheese, cake, gum, or fruit) at the crime scene. Casts of these bite marks can lead to

identifying suspects by their dentition. To make these casts complete the following steps:

    a. To preserve these bite marks, begin by painting a thin layer of liquid wax or cyanoacrylate over the bite.

    b. Repeat putting layers of wax over the bite mark and surrounding areas until there is a firm coating of wax on the food.

    c. Let the wax cool completely.

    d. Remove the wax carefully, as to not distort the impression of the bite that you have captured in the wax (Dorion 2005).

    e. When making a cast from the alginate impression of the victim's teeth, follow the same steps to make a cast from this wax impression using dental stone.

3. Styrofoam—used to be an acceptable media to make sample test bites but now it is only used as a last resort if no better material can be found.

### Impressions

1. Suspect's Dental Impression—An impression needs to be made of the suspect's teeth by completing the following steps (same steps as when making impressions of the victim's teeth):

    a. Get the correct size impression trays, one upper and one lower, depending on the mouth size of the suspect in question.

    b. Measure out the correct amount of dental alginate and put it into a plastic bowl.

    c. Pour in the appropriate amount of water into the bowl. (Follow the directions for the proper ratio of alginate and water for the dental alginate that you are using).

    d. Mix the contents until there is a smooth mixture with no clumps or air bubbles.

    e. Fill the upper and lower impression trays with the alginate mixture. Work quickly so that the alginate does not begin to set.

    f. Once the trays are filled place one in the suspect's mouth and tell the suspect to bite down hard for two minutes.

    g. Remove the tray and set it aside to finish setting.

    h. Now insert the second tray and repeat procedure.

    i. Once the alginate has set, one can move on to making the casts. Remember to leave the impressions in the trays when making the casts. These trays serve as backing for the materials (Dorion 2005).

### Casts

1. Once the impressions have been made of the suspect's teeth, casts need to be made following these steps (same steps as when making casts of the victim's teeth):

    a. Dental stone is used to make casts from the alginate impressions. Follow the instructions that come with the dental stone for the appropriate ratio of dental stone to water. First pour the dental stone powder into a plastic bowl.

b.  Add water to the bowl.
c.  Mix thoroughly to get all of the clumps out of the mixture.
d.  Fill each of the alginate impressions with dental stone mixture. Be sure to press the mixture firmly to be sure to get into all of the spaces and "nooks and crannies" created by the teeth.
e.  After the dental stone is in, tap the impressions to be sure that there are no air bubbles in the mixture.
f.  Let the cast set for about 45 minutes.
g.  After the dental stone has set, remove the cast and alginate impression from the trays. One can now peel away the alginate impression and throw it away. What is left is a cast model of the suspect's teeth that can be used for comparison purposes to the bite marks that were created (Dorion 2005).

# Methods of Comparing Bite Mark Evidence

There are numerous ways to compare a piece of bite mark evidence with a particular suspect's dentition. Many of these methods employ the use of life-size photographs of the bite mark itself. This way different techniques can be applied and compared to these photographs of the bite mark.

### Overlays (hollow volume)—outline or perimeter of each biting surface

1.  Clear acetate sheets are used to trace the suspect's dentition from the models of the teeth that were made. Two overlays are made; one for the upper teeth and one for the lower teeth. These sheets can be laid onto photographs of the bite mark to make a comparison.
2.  Today new techniques are being employed that use a computer to generate these images of the suspect's teeth that can be overlaid onto photographs of the bite mark evidence (Dorion, 2005).

### Casts

1.  Once a cast has been made of the suspect's teeth it can be used for comparison to the photographs of the bite mark evidence.
2.  The casts themselves can be placed over the photograph to see if the suspect's dentition matches up to the mark left on the victim. One can look for matches of irregularities or individual characteristics on the bite mark to the same irregularities of the suspect's teeth that could have made these unique marks (Dorion 2005).

### Comparison techniques/not using photographs

1.  Suspect's bite to excised tissue—if there has been tissue that has been removed from the victim, a direct comparison can be

made between the suspect's dental cast model to the excised bite mark tissue (Forensic Dentistry Online 2005 B).
2. A forensic dentist can also compare a suspect's dental cast model to the mold impression of the bite mark itself. The cast model of the teeth can be placed directly onto the impression of the bite mark. Then one can see if the teeth and the impression fit together meaning that a particular suspect could have made the bite mark that is on the victim (Dorion 2005).

## Description and Interpretation of Bite Marks

It is imperative that experts agree on the terminology used to describe and interpret bite marks in order to accurately relay information to attorneys, judges, juries, and other experts during the litigation process. Standardized guidelines enable the reader to grasp the knowledge necessary to preserve and compare bite marks. The American Board of Forensic Odontology (ABFO) has suggested that the following terminology contained in the ABFO Guidelines be employed in bite mark comparison.

- **Possible bite mark**—An injury showing a pattern that may or may not be caused by teeth; could be caused by other factors but biting cannot be ruled out. Criteria: general shape and size are present but distinctive features such as tooth marks are missing, incomplete, or distorted.
- **Probable bite mark**—The pattern strongly suggests or supports origin from teeth but could conceivably be caused by something else. Criteria: pattern shows some characteristics of teeth arranged around arches.
- **Definite bite mark**—There is no reasonable doubt that teeth created the pattern; other possibilities were considered and excluded. Criteria: pattern conclusively illustrates features and characteristics of dental arches and human teeth in proper arrangement so that it is recognizable as an impression of the human dentition (Forensic Dentistry Online 2005 B).

Table 4.1 is a compilation of commonly used terminology in bite mark comparisons with their connotations. However, the descriptions in Table 4.1 are not mutually exclusive. There are other appropriate descriptions in addition to the above terms which may be used by experts to describe bite marks. Table 4.2 is a compilation of additional terms used in bite mark comparisons with their connotations.

## Conclusion

As one can see, there are many different techniques employed when analyzing bite mark evidence. Once the casts, dentitions, and photographs have been made, they should be sent to the laboratory

**Table 4.1**  Bite Mark Terminology

| Ranking | Connotation |
|---|---|
| Definite, positively | No doubt in my mind it is a bite mark |
| Reasonable medical certainty, highly probable | Virtual certainty; allows for the possibility of another cause, however remote |
| Probable | More likely than not |
| Possible, similar to, consistent with, conceivable, cannot be excluded | Such a mark could have been produced by teeth but not necessarily and could have been created by something else |
| Unlikely, inconsistent, improbable | Less likely than not |
| Incompatible, excluded, impossible | No doubt in my mind it is not a bite mark; represents something else |
| Indeterminable, should not be used, insufficient | Pattern shows insufficient characterization to comment on teeth as a cause |

**Table 4.2**  Additional Common Bite Mark Terminology

| Terms | Connotation |
|---|---|
| Reasonable medical certainty, extremely probable, high degree of certainty | Virtual certainty, no reasonable or practical possibility that someone else did it |
| Very probable, probable, most unlikely | More likely than not |
| Possible, consistent, cannot exclude | Could be; may or may not be; cannot be ruled out |
| Improbable | Unlikely to be the biter |
| Ruled out, excluded, exculpatory, could not have, eliminated, dissimilar, no match, incompatible, not of common origin | Not the biter |
| Inadequate, inconclusive, insufficient | Insufficient quality/quantity/specificity of evidence to make any statement of relationship to the biter |
| Evidence has no probative (forensic) value, unsuitable | Of no evidentiary value |

for analysis. Dentists are often employed as experts in the practice of forensic odontology. They often rely on dental records to match the bite mark to suspect, although dentitions are commonly more reliable because many people do not visit the dentist on a regular basis, resulting in inaccurate dental records.

The method most often employed when comparing bite marks is the overlay method. This involves making a transparent copy, or acetate copy, of the suspect's dentition and placing it over the photograph of the bite mark located on the victim or other object. The points of pressure are compared and the bite mark will be deemed either consistent with a mark left by the suspect or the suspect will be eliminated. The actual dentition can also be placed over the actual bite mark, but oftentimes this will not be feasible because bite marks tend to disappear after a short period of time so that by the time the criminal case went to trial, the original bite mark would no longer be present.

Oftentimes, the bite mark examiner will determine the class characteristics of a mark. As mentioned previously, class characteristics, when considering bite marks, include the different types of teeth, such as incisors, molars, bicuspids, or canines, as well as whether or not the bite mark impression came from teeth on the upper or lower jaws. Incisors are thin and tend to be square shaped and, consequently, leave an impression that is very narrow and long. Canines are more pointed in nature and, therefore, leave a sharp pointed impression. Molars are square and leave impressions that reflect that shape. In addition to the specific type of tooth that formed the bite mark impression, conclusions can be drawn about whether the mark came from the upper or lower teeth. The teeth from the upper jaw create larger patterns, a direct result of their generally larger size. Also, the directionality of the U-shaped arch formed from the bite mark impression can help an analyst determine from what jaw the impression resulted (Bowers 2004).

Individual characteristics are the most useful type of characteristic when examining bite mark impressions. Teeth impressions are similar to fingerprints in that the odds of two people having the exact same bite mark impressions are minimal at best. Thus, these individual characteristics allow an examiner to eliminate suspects as well as identify a suspect from their bite mark. Alignment of an individual's teeth can help either eliminate or incriminate a suspect. A specific example of this is in the case of Ted Bundy. Bundy was wanted in connection with a multitude of murders. One of his victims from the Chi Omega sorority house in Tallahassee, Florida, sustained a bite mark to her left buttock. This would be the crucial piece of evidence that would physically connect Bundy to the crime. His lower front teeth dentition appeared to be consistent with the bruising resulting from the bite mark left on the victim and he was later convicted of the murder. Another case in which individual characteristics of a dental impression played a vital role occurred in 1967 in Scotland. Gordon Hay was convicted of murdering a 15-year-old girl based on his unique canine teeth caused by a rare disorder called hypocalcination. This particular disorder resulted in pits being formed on the teeth. These pits were clearly visible on the bite mark observed on the victim and this evidence ultimately led to his conviction (Evans 1996).

When observing bite marks on a victim it is important to note that many times objects other than teeth leave markings on the body that appear to be bite marks. These types of marks do not have any distinguishing features and are classified as "possible bite marks." They can be caused by teeth, brooches, or belt buckles and therefore, due to the lack of class and individual characteristics, a positive identification will not be able to be assessed. A definite bite mark is a mark that is positively identified as a direct result of teeth. Many characteristics are present that allow this assessment to be made accurately. This assessment is made by the qualified forensic odontologist or dentist, and because class and individual characteristics are present, care must be taken to preserve the evidence (Stimson and Mertz 1997, pp. 137–158).

The American Board of Forensic Odontology (ABFO), is the leading organization in the area of bite mark evidence. According to the ABFO, there are specific methods employed to preserve the bite mark evidence. With this particular type of evidence, this step is crucial because bite marks fade over time in live victims and therefore accurate records need to be maintained. First, saliva swabs should be taken first to acquire any DNA that the perpetrator might have left behind. Second, high quality photographs should be taken of the bite mark for use in an acetate overlay and also in the event that the actual cast of the bite mark does not process successfully. In this photograph, it is imperative that a scale be included in order to ensure that both the photograph and the comparison casts are of the same size, assisting the forensic odontologist in determining whether or not the individual characteristics of a suspect's dentition match those of the bite mark located on the victim or surface. Impressions of the bite site are then taken as well as dentitions of the victim in the case that defensive markings were made on the suspect by the victim. At times, it is necessary to excise the bite mark from the deceased victim if it cannot be accurately observed on the victim. Dentitions should be taken from the suspect in addition to saliva swabbings, when appropriate. All of these types of dental evidence are then analyzed by a forensic odontologist, often dentists, by the means mentioned earlier (Forensic Dentistry Online).

As one can see, bite mark evidence can be very useful in helping connect a suspect to a specific crime and victim. It is important that this particular type of evidence be handled with extreme care, just as with other types of evidence. Due to the fleeting nature of bite mark evidence, the processing should be performed swiftly, but the integrity of the mark should not be compromised in any way. Also, it is imperative that accurate and clear photographs be taken of the bite mark in order to further ensure the impression's reliability.

# References

BOWERS, C. M. 2004. *Forensic dental evidence: An investigator's handbook.* San Diego, CA: Elsevier.

*Daubert v. Merrell Dow Pharmaceuticals, Inc.* 1995. 516 U.S. 869., 116 S.Ct. 189., 133 L.Ed.2d 126., 64 USLW 3222., 64 USLW 3245.

DORIAN, R. (Ed.). 2005. *Bitemark evidence.* New York: Marcel Dekker.

*Doyle v. State.* 1954. 159 Tex.Crim. 310 263 S.W.2d 779.

EVANS, C. 1996. *The casebook of forensic detection: How science solved 100 of the world's most baffling crimes.* NY: John Wiley & Sons, Inc.

Forensic Dentistry Online. *ABFO bitemark guidelines.* Retrieved October 24, 2005, from http://www.forensicdentistryonline.org/bitemark_homepage.htm

Forensic Dentistry Online. 2005 A. *On-line study guides bitemarks.* Retrieved October 12, 2005, from http://www.forensicdentistryonline.org

Forensic Dentistry Online. 2005 B. *ABFO bitemark guidelines.* Retrieved September 28, 2005, from http://www.forensicdentistryonline.org

FURUHATA, T., and K. YAMAMOTO. 1967. *Forensic odontology.* Springfield, IL: Charles C. Thomas.

GLASS, R. T. 2005. Forensic odontology. In S. James and J. Nordby (Eds), *Forensic science: An introduction to scientific and investigative techniques* (2nd ed. pp. 79–98). Boca Raton, FL: CRC Press.

MCNAMEE, A., and D. SWEET. 2003 March. Adherence of forensic odontologists to the ABFO guidelines for victim evidence collection. *Journal of Forensic Sciences, 48*(2), 382–385.

MOENSSENS, A. A., and F. E. INBAU 1978. *Scientific evidence in criminal cases* (2nd ed.). Mineola, NY: The Foundation Press, Inc.

*Niehaus v. State of Indiana.* 1977. 265 Ind. 655., 359 N.E.2d 513.

*People v. Marx.* 1975. 54 Cal.App.3d 100., 126 Cal.Rptr. 350., 77 A.L.R.3d 1108.

*State v. Sager.* 1980. 600 S.W.2d 541.

STIMSON, P. G., and C. A. MERTZ. 1997. Bite mark techniques and terminology. In P. Stimson and C. Mertz (Eds.), *Forensic dentistry* (pp. 137–158). Boca Raton, FL: CRC Press.

# 5

# Toolmarks

*Anna Leggett and Sharla McCloskey*

## Introduction

On May 20, 1927, Colonel Charles A. Lindbergh was the first person to pilot an airplane across the Atlantic by himself. Almost five years later, on March 1, 1932, his son Charles Lindbergh, Junior, was kidnapped from the family home in Hopewell, New Jersey. The police arrived to search for the child and destroyed almost every piece of evidence with their carelessness. All that remained was a broken homemade ladder, apparently used by the kidnapper to climb into the child's room. More than two months later, the body of the boy was found in the woods near the Lindbergh home. Using toolmarks present on the ladder, Arthur Koehler, a carpenter and wood expert, traced a piece of wood from the ladder to the attic of Richard Hauptmann. Hauptmann was convicted for kidnapping and murder and sentenced to death based partially on the evidence presented by Koehler. This case is one of the most famous cases where toolmarks were used as evidence to lead to a conviction (Nickell and Fisher 1999).

A toolmark is an impression or scrape that is left behind when a harder object (the tool) is pressed or moved across a softer surface. The tool could be almost any relatively hard object that will leave a mark on a surface softer than itself, ranging from the more commonly known screwdriver and hammer to firearms and even teeth (Lee and Harris 2000). Some of the more common tools are depicted in Figure 5.1. The type of surface on which a toolmark is left greatly affects the quality of the mark. Tools leave high-quality markings on plastics and soft metals, such as copper, lead, and brass, but striations naturally present in wooden surfaces make it difficult to compare toolmarks made in them. Additionally, hard metals, such as carbonized steel, do not generally respond as well to the pressure and force of the tool. As a result, it is very difficult for the tool to leave a mark on this type of surface (Rowe 2005).

Toolmarks are typically discovered near points of entry at crime scenes, like doors and windows, and near any place where valuables might be kept, such as safes and locked drawers (De Forest, Gaensslen, and Lee 1983). Many different types of toolmarks may be

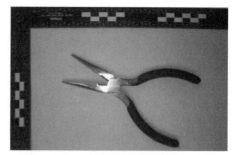

**Figure 5.1**  Common Types of Tools: Hammer and Needle-Nose Pliers

found on safes because of the variety of ways to break into them. For example, the doors of some safes can be pried open or even attacked with an electric drill. Toolmarks may also be made on locks and chain link fences by bolt or wire cutters (Rowe 2005).

There are two major types of toolmarks: indentations and striations. *Indentations*, also called impression and compression marks, occur when the tool is pushed forcefully against another object such that a negative impression of the tool remains on the surface. This is similar to the impressions left behind by tires and shoes. One example of an indentation would be the mark of a hammer in a soft wooden surface. The details of the hammer's head or claw would be visible in the wood. Figures 5.2 and 5.3 demonstrate toolmarks made by a hammer in a doorframe.

*Striations*, also referred to as sliding or scraping marks, occur when a tool is forced to move across a surface. The markings on the surface exhibit a series of parallel lines that follow the direction of motion of the tool. An example of this type of mark would be the scraping of a crowbar against a metal surface (De Forest, et al. 1983). In some circumstances, such as marks made by cutting tools, both indentations and striations might be present. For example, as a saw cuts through a wooden surface, it leaves an indentation in the wood, as well as striations along the surface. Some forensic scientists classify this as a separate distinct category of toolmarks (Rowe 2005).

As with other areas of forensic identification, toolmarks can be identified according to class and individual characteristics. Class characteristics involve the type of tool used to make the mark. These include the size and shape of the tool and the distance between teeth on a serrated instrument such as a saw (Schehl 2000). Certain striation patterns that are common to a specific type of tool can also be called class characteristics. Class characteristics are identical when the tools are of the same type and manufactured with the same process (Rowe 2005).

On the other hand, differences in the production processes of the tool and damage caused by wear or mishandling of the tool create individual characteristics. These characteristics are unique to a single tool and the same combination of individual characteristics will most likely not be found with any other tool. Positive identification of the tool is based on matching both class and individual

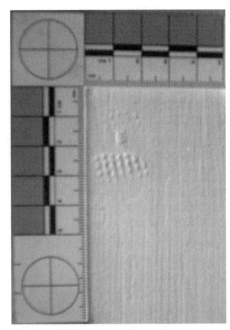

**Figure 5.2**    Toolmark Made in a Doorframe by the Head of a Hammer

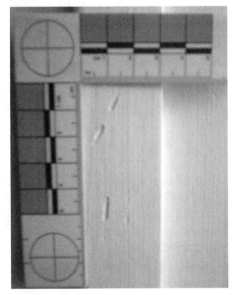

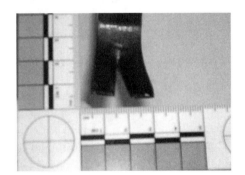

**Figure 5.3**    Toolmarks in a Doorframe Made by the Claw of the Hammer Pictured

characteristics. A negative match between two tools occurs when the class characteristics of the tools are declared significantly different (Rowe 2005).

Toolmarks can also be a significant source of trace evidence. Paint, hair, fibers, body fluids, and many other substances could have adhered to the surface of the tool prior to or during the actual crime. This evidence could be traced from the tool to a suspect and is an important part of toolmark examination. Additionally, fingerprints could remain on the toolmark and these could be used to identify the criminal if properly processed prior to handling (Kubic and Petraco 2005).

Toolmarks that occur during manufacturing processes can also be used during forensic examination. As plastic film, bags, and wrap are made, striations are produced on the layers of plastic. These striations are caused by calendaring or smoothing of the plastic sheet between large rollers or by extrusion of the plastic bag or film through a circular die. These striations can be analyzed using Schlieren optics or polarization to determine thickness, density, and refractive indexes of the plastic. Toolmarks on tablets of illegal drugs can also be analyzed when the drugs have been molded or made by pressing between two punches. The instrument that compresses the pills could have defects in the molding or the punches and when the pills are made, the defects are transferred to the pills. The imperfections in the pill can be viewed as a toolmark made by the instrument used to manufacture it (Rowe 2005).

The crime scene investigator should be trained to look for toolmarks at all types of crime scenes. They should document the location of the toolmark, the date it was found, and the name of the investigator who found it, as well as take distance and close-up photographs of the mark. Additionally, the investigator should search for possible tools that could have made the mark in and around the area of the crime scene. After the initial analysis and documentation, the toolmark should be removed from the scene if possible and transported to the crime lab.

## Operating and Lifting Procedures

### *Photographic Evidence*

At a crime scene, toolmarks should be carefully documented and preserved before transporting the evidence to a lab. Before any other crime scene processing takes place, photographs must be taken. After the initial photos are taken that portray the entire crime scene, general photos should be taken of any toolmarks found. The dimensions of the toolmarks and their location should always be noted on the crime scene sketch, and location should be visible within the first photos taken of the actual toolmark. Because toolmarks are usually not located on the floor, the investigator must be careful to also measure the distance from the floor and/or ceiling to the toolmark. Photos of toolmarks should be structured so that the area of the crime scene where the toolmarks are located show a clear view of the toolmark and its placement. Next, detailed photos should be taken of the toolmark. These should be taken at close ranges using the zoom feature of the camera to ensure that as much detail as possible can be seen in the photos. A ruler with clear, readable graduations should be placed in the photo to preserve the dimensions of the toolmark during later analysis or during alteration of the photo. These close-up photos can later be used for analysis if the toolmark itself or the cast of the toolmark becomes unusable. These photos may become the only actual record of the toolmark evidence present at the crime scene (Nickell and Fisher 1999).

If possible a video camera should be used to document all of the evidence within the crime scene. A video should exhibit a continual, careful walk-through of the crime scene. The video should start with the date and time of commencement and location of the crime scene, preferably written on a card large enough to be viewed by the camera and read aloud. Also, throughout the documentation process, the accurate date and time should be displayed on the screen. The only audio necessary is the narration of the progression through the crime scene. This video can be done in conjunction with or prior to the general photography of the crime scene. (Schiro n.d.)

The accurate maintenance of chain of custody is essential in crime scene analysis. Chain of custody is the documentation of the evidence. It begins when the evidence is collected at the crime scene. The chain of custody is maintained at all times through the investigation process and can involve crime scene analysts, lab personnel, prosecuting attorneys, and police persons. It is the job of the crime scene investigator to initiate the chain of custody by documenting where and when the evidence is found. This begins with the photography, which documents the initial finding of the evidence. Throughout the photography process, the investigator should be documenting the location of photos taken, their numbers on the roll of film, and a short description of what is in each photograph.

## Toolmark Processing

After all photographic evidence has been acquired; the toolmark itself can begin to be processed. During all crime scene processing, examination or latex gloves should be worn. This helps to preserve evidence integrity while minimizing contamination. At the scene of the crime an investigator or police person should never attempt to fit any tool into a toolmark. This could potentially modify or destroy the toolmark and can later be used by defense attorneys to discredit the evidence. Also, if tool-to-toolmark matching is attempted at the crime scene, any trace evidence that may be present in the toolmark can be compromised or destroyed. Any tool found during crime scene processing should be identified with its location and method of discovery. If the discovered tool fits the profile for the toolmark, it should be kept separate from the toolmark and transported to the appropriate laboratory for processing. The correct handling and transportation of toolmark evidence and tools collected at crime scenes will be discussed later. The main goal of crime scene investigation concerning toolmarks is their preservation for later analysis. (Garrison and Green n.d.)

## Trace Evidence

The first step in the analysis of a toolmark should be an examination for trace evidence such as paint, glass, metal, blood, and especially latent fingerprints. Depending on the quality of the fingerprint, a decision must be made as to which evidence to collect: the latent fingerprint or the other trace evidence present. However, both fingerprint and other trace evidence should be collected when possible. Before attempting to develop a latent print, any "loosely adhering" trace evidence can be collected, packaged, and labeled for submission. The latent print can then be developed and lifted. During the trace evidence analysis, care must be taken not to destroy or alter the toolmark (California Department of Justice 1984). When trace evidence is collected, it should be placed in envelopes and labeled with location, date, and name and/or initials of the examiner to preserve chain of custody.

Within the arena of the trace evidence, there exist two types of evidence. Trace can refer to evidence like fibers, paint, scrapings, and any unidentifiable evidence. Trace evidence can also be residue transferred from the tool to the mark or vice versa. Residue evidence comes from interaction between the tool and the other objects. This evidence includes oils or dirt and grime that come from everyday use. This type of trace comes from prior use of the tool and is not collected at the scene. It is preserved on the tool by careful handling and transported to the lab for analysis.

After unidentified trace evidence is collected from the toolmark, standards or substances of known origin should be collected from the area around the toolmark. These include scrapings of paint from the area where the toolmark is located, and should be taken from the wall, door, or ceiling if it is suspected that the tool may have come into contact with the surface. Samples of insulation and other building materials from a damaged wall should be collected as well. Any liquids that are near the area of the mark should also be collected and retained as standards. For toolmarks located on human skin, trace evidence would include any fiber and hair samples that could be obtained at the time of processing. This known trace evidence should be placed in different types of containers than the collected trace evidence and should be labeled with date, crime scene information, and location of collection (California Department of Justice 1984). Usually, glass vials are used to hold this type of evidence because it is distinctively different and can be easily labeled. Because photos are essential to the crime scene investigation, it is recommended that the location of the standard collection be photographed and documented both before and after collection.

## Toolmark Processing

After all available trace evidence has been collected and documented, the processing of the actual toolmark can begin. If at all possible, the object on which the toolmark was made or the actual toolmark itself should be removed from the crime scene and submitted for analysis.

### Small Objects

Toolmarks made on objects that can be easily transported should always be removed from the crime scene and submitted to the appropriate lab for analysis. Objects of easy mobility are objects, for example, not part of the structure of a house or a person, but evidence that can be removed from the crime scene and transported to the lab without causing significant damage to personal property.

### Large Objects

For toolmarks on large objects, such as door frames, doors, and so on, the area containing the toolmark should be cut out and submitted for analysis. When determining whether to remove a toolmark from the crime scene located on a large object, the evidentiary value of the toolmark must substantially outweigh the value of damage caused to the object from where the toolmark will be removed. The area removed should be large enough to prevent any damage to the toolmark during the removal process and later transportation. When the toolmark is being removed, it should be loosely covered to prevent any wood shavings or other cast-off of the process from becoming imbedded in the mark and altering details. Before removal, the directionality of the mark, including top and front of the item, should be noted within the area; it may also be helpful to photograph the toolmark with notations before and then again after (Byrd 2000).

### Attached Toolmarks

Toolmarks made by wire or bolt cutters are often found on the ends of wires, cables, and other similar objects. Because they are usually a part of a larger system of wires, they can be tough to preserve. To collect this evidence, the wire with the toolmark would need to be removed by the crime scene analyst before transport can take place. Usually, 6 to 12 inches of wire or cable is a manageable and sufficient length for removal. In these cases, the analyst would need to use tools not associated with the crime scene to cut the wire from the larger system. Before any cutting takes place, the end of the object attached to the toolmark must be wrapped by brown paper or covered by an envelope to preserve trace evidence. Then, a portion of the wire can be removed. Before the actual separation is carried out, the end to be cut by the analyst must be labeled to prevent a mix-up later on. The tool used for removing the wire would need to be submitted to casting for standards purposes (Lee and Harris 2000).

### Cleaning Toolmarks

After all trace evidence has been collected from the toolmark, it must be cleaned before casting can take place. The cleaning of a toolmark should only be done with a solution of high volatility (a solution that evaporates quickly like acetone) that will allow for a short amount of time until the toolmark is dry. The toolmark should not be cleaned with any type of brush because this has the potential of altering the details of the toolmark.

# Toolmarks and the Human Body

### Bone

Toolmarks can be found on any type of material that will keep an impression. This includes parts of the human body such as bones and skin. These toolmarks in bone are found on cross sections of bones or as impressions on the skull. They are usually a result of sawing or what is termed as *hacking trauma.* Hacking trauma is inflicted by chopping tools or weapons, such as machetes, axes, and cleavers on a body that leaves striations in the bone that correspond to the striations on the cutting edge of the instrument (Tucker et al. 2001). An easily identifiable or highly suspicious toolmark at a crime scene, such as those on bone should automatically be photographed, cataloged, collected as evidence, and preserved for later analysis. No attempt to cast a toolmark on bone at a crime scene should be attempted.

The main concern when handling toolmarks in bone is the fragility of the bone. Bone collection at crime scenes should preferably be handled by an anthropologist. However, usually the same person is attempting to preserve all the evidence at a single crime scene. No attempt at a crime scene should be made to clean the bones or to reassemble them into working order. They should be packaged as separately as possible. The bones that are suspected of having toolmarks should be marked on the outside of the evidence containers; however, later examination should include all recovered bones for toolmarks.

### Skin

Toolmarks on skin are often a result of mutilation or torture inflicted upon the victim. Because the human skin is very resilient and tends to bounce back from injury, especially in living victims, it is important to cast the toolmark as quickly as possible. For these types of toolmarks, it is preferable to cast the toolmark directly from the skin. It is a plausible option for a medical examiner to remove a portion of skin and/or tissue for later analysis but not a crime scene analyst. First, nothing should be removed from a body prior to autopsy. Second, when taken out of context (the body), the skin tends to lose shape and the exact striations or impressions from the tool can be lost. Again, photograph, catalog, collect, and preserve the evidence for later analysis.

# Casting Toolmarks

If the area containing the toolmark cannot be submitted for analysis, the toolmark must be cast at the scene. Most casting materials, such as dental stone, come as a powder that can be mixed with water to form a liquid mixture that is poured into the impression and allowed to harden. These types of casting materials are useful for toolmarks found on floors or the bottom of windowsills. However, a great number of toolmarks at crime scenes are not in easily accessible or reasonable areas in the crime scene, but are often found on objects that are not flat on the ground or are not situated on a horizontal surface. To cast impressions made vertically, casting materials with higher viscosities are necessary. It is possible to mix dental stone with less than the recommended amount of water so that it will be thicker, but the problem still persists of maintaining a form around the toolmark until the cast begins to harden. Also, the detail necessary to accurately analyze a toolmark will not be present from thick dental stone. Therefore, most toolmark castings are made from high-resolution silicone rubber materials, such as Mikrosil™. Silicone rubber casting is the most efficient casting material to use for toolmarks as it gives a higher resolution than either plaster of Paris or dental stone (California Department of Justice 1984).

Most silicone casting materials come in kits that have easy-to-follow instructions of mixing and application. After the casting material has been mixed, the mixture is applied directly to a clean toolmark and allowed to set. A tongue depressor can be used to mix and smooth the casting material leaving the tongue depressor in the mixture as it dries. This will give the investigator a place to label the cast with all the necessary information needed for cataloging and later identification. Because writing will not stay permanently on silicone, the depressor can be labeled and then later used as a handle for removal of the cast. If the depressor is left in the mixture it should be placed parallel to the casting surface with the flat side facing out. It should also be deep enough to be used as a handle but not deep enough to alter the casting of the toolmark (Byrd 2000).

Casting materials usually require 30 to 40 minutes to dry and harden, but each material is different and all instructions come with drying time specifications. When the casting material is hard and cool to the touch, it is usually ready to be removed. The cast should then be carefully pried away from the toolmark. If the cast begins to distort or break it should gently be placed back into position and allowed to complete the hardening process. The cast should then be placed into an evidence box. This box will be labeled with collector's name, date, and crime scene and then cataloged to preserve chain of custody.

### Packaging and Transportation

After the toolmark evidence has been collected, it must then be packaged in a way to preserve its evidentiary and scientific integrity. All casts should be loosely wrapped in paper, for example, brown paper grocery bags, and then placed inside an appropriately sized box, which has been labeled and cataloged to preserve chain of custody, for transport. Evidence boxes are sturdy, but care must still be taken when packing multiple boxes for transport. Pack heaviest to lightest from bottom to top.

## Conclusion

Once the toolmark evidence has been collected from the crime scene and transported to a lab facility, forensic scientists must analyze it to determine the tool that made the mark. The types of toolmarks found, whether impressions or striations, are analyzed using different methods. The first technique for evaluating impression evidence involves the actual tool and the indentation found at the crime scene. This process can be difficult because the mark is a negative image of the actual tool, and the forensic scientist must prove that the tool created the mark (De Forest et al. 1983).

> Because of the difficulties of comparing the actual tool to the mark it made, the second method is most often used in the examination of impression evidence. This approach involves making test impressions of the toolmark and comparing these impressions to ones made at the crime scene. Test marks should generally be produced in a material very similar to that found at the crime scene. However, when the crime scene surface is very hard, impressions may be made first in a softer material to protect the tool from any damage. The exact conditions of the toolmark made at the crime scene must be reproduced, specifically the angle and depth at which the original mark was made. (De Forest et al. 1983)

Different techniques are employed to analyze striated toolmarks. The striations on the crime scene mark must be exactly matched to the suspected tool. When toolmark examiners investigate striations, they are most concerned with the height and the width of the striae because the length of the striae depends only on the amount of time the tool was in contact with the surface. The striated markings left on the material are a negative image of the tool that made the marks: the valleys of the mark correspond to protrusions on the tool while the hills of the mark match indentations present on the tool. After test marks are made of the striae, the markings are compared to the crime scene striae through the use of a comparison microscope (Davis 1958). An example of toolmark comparison is shown in Figure 5.4.

This microscope involves two compound microscopes that are connected so that two samples can be analyzed in the same view frame. A thin line in the frame separates the images of the test marks and the crime scene toolmarks. The test marks and the actual marks can be moved independently of each other, and the two compound microscopes are adjusted to make the lighting on each specimen the same. If the toolmarks came from the same tool, the marks will appear to continue through both frames; however, if the samples do not match, the striations will abruptly end at the line separating the samples. Using oblique lighting techniques, an estimate can be made of the height and width of the striae in each sample, but it is generally difficult to obtain precise results using this method (Davis 1958).

The Striagraph, an instrument created in 1950, was designed to analyze the surfaces of toolmarks and fired bullets using mechanical and optical technology. This apparatus creates tracings of

**Figure 5.4**   Comparison Microscope Analysis of Toolmarks
*Photo Credit: Courtesy of Maine Crime Lab. Used with permission.*

both flat and cylindrical surfaces to demonstrate the contours present. Striated toolmarks, either the actual mark or a plastic impression, can be analyzed using the Striagraph. This instrument enables detailed and accurate contour analysis of the toolmark that may reveal subtle differences that would not normally be detectable using a microscope. The initial analysis is still done with the comparison microscope but for some toolmarks, it is important to use the Striagraph to demonstrate height and depth of the striae, as well as location and waviness of the actual mark. The Striagraph can also be used to determine stamped serial numbers in impression marks that cannot be read in other analyses (Davis 1958). More recently, Heizmann and Leon (2001) have developed an automated technique using computers to determine the specific signature of the grooves left behind by a tool or firearm.

Scanning electron microscopes (SEM) have been recently used to analyze hacking traumas in bones from knives and hatchets. This technique is usually employed to analyze smaller marks that are not easily distinguished with an investigator's eye. In order to analyze toolmarks on human bone with SEM, the toolmark must be isolated on a portion of bone smaller than 1 centimeter square and then covered with a thin layer of gold. Analysis with the SEM produces highly magnified pictures of the mark that show incredible detail and enable the investigator to determine more individual and class characteristics. After more thorough research has been conducted, the use of the SEM will hopefully be applied to other types of toolmarks that are difficult to analyze (Alunni-Perrett et al. 2005).

To determine the class characteristics of a tool, measurements of the toolmark must be made to determine the size of the tool that created it. If the toolmark is an impression, measurements can give the examiner an estimate of the shape and type of the tool. With striations, usually only the width of the tool that made the mark can be determined. However, certain striation patterns could be characteristic of a type of tool, such as slip-joint pliers, and may be considered class characteristics. The striations present on needle-nose pliers can be seen in Figure 5.5. The pattern of these striations would be a class characteristic because it is common among all needle-nose pliers made by the same manufacturer (Rowe 2005).

Individual characteristics can be identified by imperfections in the tool that made the mark. Manufacturing processes could lead to these imperfections. For example, bolt cutters and wire cutters are usually sharpened on a grinding wheel while they are being made. Because this process is done manually, the striations on each tool are different and could be used to identify the exact tool that created the mark. Also, unique characteristics on a tool could result from damage caused by the user. This kind of damage could occur when a person uses a saw incorrectly and as a result, the teeth of the saw become bent or broken. The patterns found when that saw was used at a crime scene would be different than a saw that was recently purchased. The circular shape of a hammer's head and the impressions on the face of the head could be changed slightly by pounding at different angles, resulting in individual characteristics (Rowe 2005).

For each toolmark found at a crime scene, both class and individual characteristics must be determined so that the mark can be compared to tools either found at crime scenes or obtained from suspects. There is a positive identification when both class and individual characteristics match between a test mark and the crime scene mark. There is a negative identification if the class characteristics of the two marks do not match, and the results are inconclusive if only class characteristics match without individual characteristics (Rowe 2005). There is no specific number of characteristics that must match for toolmark comparisons (De Forest et al. 1983).

Toolmark examinations are usually conducted by analysts in a firearms lab. As with tools, the manufacturing process of many

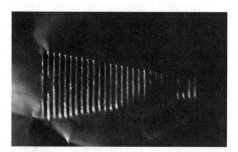

**Figure 5.5** Striations Made by Needle-Nose Pliers on Aluminum Foil

firearms results in the unique characteristics of the weapon. As the weapon is fired, these characteristics can be transferred to the bullet, cartridge case, or other ammunition component. The bullet generally receives marks from the chamber of the firearm, including the grooves of the chamber as well as other individual marks present on the inside of the barrel that were caused by manufacturing or previous discharge of the gun. After a firearm has been discharged, the cartridge case will also exhibit marks from the gun, such as firing pin impressions, extractor marks, ejector marks, breechface marks, and chamber marks. Additionally, when guns are discharged at close range, the impression of the end of the firearm could be left on the skin of the victim. As with toolmarks, marks made by firearms can be classified as individual and class characteristics. A suspected firearm would be discharged in a firing range that contains a water tank and the bullet and cartridge could then be compared with the bullet or cartridge from the crime scene using a comparison microscope (Schehl 2000).

Both toolmark and firearm examinations are important aspects of forensic science. Trace evidence and fingerprints can be lifted from suspect tools, and impressions and striations can be matched to those found at crime scenes. Although analysis of firearms is much more prevalent in modern crime labs, traditional tools should not be overlooked because they can provide valuable information about the crime.

# References

ALUNNI-PERRET, V., M. MULLER-BOLLA, J. LAUGIER, L. LUPI-PEGURIER, M. BERTRAND, P. STACCINI, M. BOLLA, and G. QUATREHOMME. 2005. Scanning electron microscopy analysis of experimental bone hacking trauma. *Journal of Forensic Sciences, 50*(4).

BYRD, M. 2000. *Crime scene investigations—other impression evidence.* Miami-Dade Police Department, Crime Scene Investigations. Retrieved October 13, 2005, from http://crime-scene-investigator.net

California Department of Justice, Bureau of Forensic Services. 1984. Toolmark evidence collection. Publication No. 27. CA: Physical Evidence Bulletin.

DAVIS, J. E. 1958. *An introduction to tool marks, firearms, and the striagraph.* Springfield, IL: Charles C. Thomas.

DE FOREST, P. R., R. E. GAENSSLEN, and H. C. LEE. 1983. *Forensic science: An introduction to criminalistics.* NY: McGraw Hill, Inc.

GARRISON, T., and K. GREEN. n.d. Missouri State Highway Patrol—Crime Laboratory Division. *A Closer Examination from the Benchtop—Under the Scope, A Current Educational Bulletin for Submitting Law Enforcement Agencies.*

HEIZMANN, M., and F. P. LEON. 2001. Automated analysis and comparison of striated toolmarks. *European meeting for shoeprint/ toolmark examiners 2001.* Retrieved October 25, 2005, from http://www.ies. uni-karlsruhe.de/download/publ/hzm/ sptm2001_pp.pdf

KUBIC, T. A., and N. PETRACO. 2005. Chapter 16: Microanalysis and examination of trace evidence. In S. James and J. Nordby (Eds.), *Forensic science: An introduction to scientific and investigative techniques* (pp. 315–340). Boca Raton, FL: CRC Press.

LEE, H. C., and H. A. HARRIS. 2000. *Physical evidence in forensic science.* Tucson, AZ: Lawyers & Judges Publishing Co., Inc.

NICKELL, J., and J. F. FISHER. 1999. *Crime science: Methods of forensic detection.* Lexington, KY: University Press of Kentucky.

ROWE, W. F. 2005. Chapter 20: Firearm and toolmark examinations. In S. James and J. Nordby (Eds.), *Forensic science: An introduction to scientific and investigative techniques* (pp. 391–421). Boca Raton, FL: CRC Press.

SCHEHL, S. A. 2000. Firearms and toolmarks in the FBI laboratory, part 2. *Forensic Science Communications, 2*(2). Retrieved October 25, 2005, from http://www.fbi.gov/

SCHIRO, GEORGE. n.d. The Texas investigator. Collection and preservation of evidence: Part 1 & 3. Retrieved October 24, 2005 from www.tali.org/texasinv/evidence.htm

TUCKER, B. K., D. L. HUTCHINSON, M. F. GILLILAND, T. M. CHARLES, and H. J. DANIEL. 2001. Microscopic characteristics of hacking trauma. *Journal of Forensic Sciences, 46*(2), 234–240.

# Further Reading

ANDAHL, R. O. 1978. The examination of saw marks. *The Journal of the Forensic Science Society, 18*, 31–46.

BROWN, S., A. KLEIN, and A. CHAIKOVSKY. 2003. Deciphering indented impressions on plastic. *Journal of Forensic Sciences, 48*(4), 1–5.

DAVIS, R. J. 1981. An intelligence approach to footwear marks and toolmarks. *The Journal of the Forensic Science Society, 21*, 183–194.

DU PASQUIER, E., J. HEBRARD, P. MARGOT, and M. INEICHEN. 1996. Evaluation and comparison of casting materials in forensic sciences, applications to toolmarks and foot/shoe impressions. *Forensic Science International, 82*, 33–43.

HEIZMANN, M., and F. P. LEON. 2000. Model-based analysis of striation patterns in forensic science. *International Symposium on Law Enforcement Technologies 2000.* Retrieved October 25, 2005, from http://www.ies.uni-karlsruhe.de/

LIUKKONEN, M., H. MAJAMAA, and H. VIRTANEN. 1996. The role and duties of the shoeprint/toolmark examiner in forensic laboratories. *Forensic Science International, 82*, 99–108.

MAY, L. S. 1930. The identification of knives, tools, and instruments, a positive science. *The American Journal of Police Science, 1*, 246–259.

MEZGER, O., F. HASSLACHER, and P. FRANKLE. 1930. Identification of marks made on trees. *The American Journal of Police Science, 1*, 358–365.

NICHOLS, R. G. 2003. Firearm and toolmark identification criteria: A review of the literature, part II. *Journal of Forensic Science 48*(2), 1–10.

POPE, E. J., and SMITH, O. C. 2004. Identification of traumatic injury in burned cranial bone: An experimental approach. *Journal of Forensic Science, 49*(3), 1–10.